Hamlet's Dreams: The Robben Island Shakespeare

Shakespeare Now!
Series edited by Ewan Fernie and Simon Palfrey
Web editors: Theodora Papadopoulou and William McKenzie

First Wave:
At the Bottom of Shakespeare's Ocean Steve Mentz
Godless Shakespeare Eric S. Mallin
Shakespeare's Double Helix Henry S. Turner
Shakespeare Inside Amy Scott-Douglass
Shakespearean Metaphysics Michael Witmore
Shakespeare's Modern Collaborators Lukas Erne
Shakespeare Thinking Philip Davis
To Be Or Not To Be Douglas Bruster

Second Wave:
The King and I Philippa Kelly
The Life in the Sonnets David Fuller
Hamlet's Dreams David Schalkwyk
Nine Lives of William Shakespeare Graham Holderness
Shakespeare and I edited by Theodora Papadopoulou and William McKenzie

Visit the *Shakespeare Now!* Blog at http://shakespearenowseries.blogspot.com/ for further news and updates on the series.

Hamlet's Dreams: The Robben Island Shakespeare

David Schalkwyk

The Arden Shakespeare

1 3 5 7 9 10 8 6 4 2

First published in 2013 by The Arden Shakespeare

The Arden Shakespeare is an imprint of Bloomsbury Publishing Plc

The Arden Shakespeare
Bloomsbury Publishing Plc
49–51 Bedford Square
London WC1B 3DP

www.ardenshakespeare.com

Hardback ISBN: 9781441140333
Paperback ISBN: 9781441129284
EPUB ISBN: 9781441110732
EPDF ISBN: 9781441183743

Available in the USA from Bloomsbury Academic & Professional,
175 Fifth Avenue/3rd Floor, New York, NY 10010.

A CIP catalogue record for this book is available from the British Library

This book is produced using paper that is made from wood grown in managed, sustainable forests. It is natural, renewable and recyclable. The logging and manufacturing processes conform to the environmental regulations of the country of origin.

In memoriam

Stephen Watson, colleague
and friend, 1954–2011

Contents

General Editors' Preface to the Second-Wave of the Series viii

Preface x

Introduction: Home and Away 1

1. 'This Island's Mine' 25
2. Hamlet's Dreams 74
3. Friendship and Struggle 120

Notes 160

Bibliography 179

Index 185

General Editors' Preface to the Second-Wave of the Series

We begin with the passions of the critic as they are forged and explored in Shakespeare. These books speak directly from that fundamental experience of losing and remaking yourself in art. This does not imply, necessarily, a lonely existentialism; the story of a self is always bound up in other stories, shared tales of nations or faiths or of families large and small. But such stories are also always singular, irreducible to the generalities by which they are typically explained. Here, then, is where literary experience stops pretending to institutionalized objectivity, and starts to tell its own story.

Shakespeare Now! is a rallying cry, above all for aesthetic immediacy. It favours a model of aesthetic knowledge as *encounter*, where the encounter brings its own, often surprising contextualizing imperatives. Implicit in this is the premise that art is as much a subject as an object, less like aggregated facts and more like a fascinating person or persons. And encountering the plays as such is unavoidably personal.

Much recent scholarship has been devoted to Shakespeare *then* – to producing more information about the presumed moment of their inception. But this moment of inception is in truth happening over and over, again and again, anywhere that Shakespeare is being experienced anew or freshly. For the fact is that he remains, by a country mile, the most important *contemporary* writer – the most performed and read, the most written about, but also the most remembered. But it is not a question merely of Shakespeare in the present, as though his vitality is best measured by his passing relevance to great events. It is about his works' abiding *presence*.

In some ways criticism needs to get younger – to recover the freshness of aesthetic experience, and so in part better to remember why any of us should care. We need a new directness, written responses to the plays which attest to the life we find in them and the life they find in us.

Ewan Fernie and Simon Palfrey

Preface

Had you visited London during the summer of 2012 and attended, in addition to the myriad of sports events during the Olympic Games, the British Library exhibition, 'Shakespeare: Staging the World', you would have encountered a curious exhibit at the very end. This last item is a somewhat scruffy, modern volume, cheaply produced, with large initials crudely inscribed in pencil along the edge of its pages. The book is like something that many readers might have held in their own hands, perhaps have in their bookshelves or recall from their parents' collection. It is surprisingly modest compared to the items that precede it: the splendid portrait of the ambassador to England from the King of Barbary; or hand D (attributed to Shakespeare) in the manuscript of the play, *Sir Thomas More*; the splendid tapestry map of Warwickshire; sixteenth-century Venetian glass; the mummified eye of the Jesuit priest, Edward Oldcorne; or even the battered latern associated with Guy Fawkes's ill-fated plot to blow up the Houses of Parliament in 1605.

The book, given pride of place precisely by virtue of being the final statement of the exhibition, received an enormous amount of publicity from newspapers and websites around the world, being picked out as the 'prize' exhibit in an extraordinarily rich collection.[1] It is *The Alexander Text of the Complete Works of Shakespeare*: probably the most widely sold and read scholarly edition of Shakespeare's texts in the twentieth century. It has sold tens of thousands of copies since its publication in 1951, and it has been reprinted some 50 times in as many years. Sometimes twice in one year.

[1] 'Banged-up bard', www.bbc.co.uk/news/entertainment-arts-18882252 (accessed 17 August 2012).

The volume on display in the British Museum is the 1970 imprint. What makes it so special? It is the so-called Robben Island Shakespeare (also known as the 'Robben Island Bible'), the property of a South African, Sonny Venkatrathnam. A political prisoner on Robben Island during the 1970s, Venkatratham was able to keep and circulate his copy of Shakespeare's works in the prison by persuading his warders that it was a religious Hindu text. He passed the book to a number of his fellow prisoners in the single cells. Each prisoner was asked to mark his favourite passage, and some signed their passage with the date. The Robben Island Shakespeare is marked by 34 signatories, each of whom we shall encounter in the pages of *Hamlet's Dreams*. The page on which Venkatrathnam's Shakespeare was open for display in London was signed on the 16th of December 1977, with the name 'N. R. Mandela'. The passage? – 'Cowards die many times before their deaths/The valiant never taste of death but once' (*Julius Caesar*, 2.2.32–3).[2]

I first came across the Robben Island Shakespeare on a visit to Stratford-upon-Avon in the summer of 2006, where it was also the final item in an exhibition in Nash House called 'Shakespeare – The Complete Works'. As in London, it was open on the page signed by Nelson Mandela. My unexpected encounter with this book in Shakespeare's birthplace – shrine of Bardolators, engine room of Shakespearean theatre and respected centre of Shakespeare scholarship – brought together two interests that, as a member of the English Departments of the Rand Afrikaans University and the University of Cape Town, I had been working on for some 20 years, although I had always kept them strictly apart: Shakespeare and South African prison writing. My first, urgent desire in this unexpected encounter was to see what this unique volume of Shakespeare comprehended: I wanted to see not merely what page Mandela had signed, but also

[2] A picture of the page appears on page 269 of Jonathan Bate and Dora Thornton, *Shakespeare: Staging the World* (Oxford: Oxford University Press, 2012).

which passages others had chosen and who the others were. My appeal to the museum guard to be allowed – on the grounds of my scholarly credentials and my nationality – to remove it from its case and peruse it was, of course, rejected with bewildered indignation. That was understandable.

Fortunately I was not in Stratford as a mere tourist. After years of waiting, I had that year finally made it onto the list of invitees to the biannual International Shakespeare Conference at Stratford – a meeting of established Shakespeare scholars and critics arranged by the Shakespeare Institute of the University of Birmingham, which has its premises in Church Street. I therefore approached Stanley Wells, former Director of the Shakespeare Institute and now Chairman of the Shakespeare Birthplace Trust, which had presented the Nash House exhibition, to ask whether I could examine the book. I could. If I went to the museum at closing time, I would be permitted to spend half an hour with Robben Island Shakespeare, Stanley told me that evening. I am very grateful to him for this kindness. Not knowing whether I would see the book again, I thought 30 minutes paltry – to record all the names (most barely legible) and the chosen passages. I worked feverishly, and was only half way through when the figure in blue loomed over me. He did, after all, need to go home. I handed back the Shakespeare. When he saw my crestfallen look he said: 'Are you looking for a list of all the gentlemen who signed the book, sir?' Yes, that would be wonderful. 'Well we do have one here, sir. Happy to copy it for you.' So I left with my precious list, and for once my scepticism of all forms of veneration of objects disappeared. There was indeed something special about having touched and read the book that had passed through the hands of the people who had saved my country. Especially striking, as I paged through it, were the desiccated Eucalyptus leaves, still bearing the faintest trace of their scent, and wild flowers pressed between its pages. They had presumably been picked on the way to the quarries where the prisoners had been subjected to hard labour, and were preserved by this Shakespeare as a tiny form of sensory richness – a reminder of the outside to be savoured and recalled. They were still there 30 years later. Shakespeare is important, I thought, but he's not everything.

My stumbling on the Robben Island Shakespeare was the first of a series of happy coincidences and serendipitous events. Had the International Shakespeare Conference not been held that year; had I not been invited; had the Shakespeare Birthday Trust not happened to have exhibited Venkatrathnam's Shakespeare at the very time I was in Stratford (that exhibit was changed every 6 months);[3] had Nash House not been in Church Street on my way back from lunch to Mason Croft; had Stanley Wells not interceded on my behalf; had the man at the museum not offered me a copy of the list . . . well, I would have had no material for my inaugural lecture as a Professor at the University of Cape Town that year, and this book would not have been written.

I had put off the rite-de-passage of the inaugural lecture for about 3 years, until I finally received a letter from the deputy Vice-Chancellor telling me that I should deliver my lecture within 6 months or forego it altogether. I had postponed the lecture in part because I had found it extremely difficult to present myself – what I 'professed' – to a general audience in a way that would both engage them and make my work relevant to its wider context. The discovery of the Robben Island Bible permitted me to do both. Its existence was known by only a handful of South Africans, and it allowed me to bring together two parts of my academic life that I had felt, until then, were intellectually irreconcilable. I gave the lecture on 26 October 2006, some 3 months after my first, unanticipated journey up the stairs in Nash House.

In 2009 I left South Africa to take up the position of Director of Research at the Folger Shakespeare Library. The Robben Island Shakespeare continued to haunt me. Colleagues in South Africa,

[3] Private conversation with Stanley Wells and Paul Edmondson at the 60th anniversary celebration of the Shakespeare Institute in November 2011.

Brian Pierce and Laurence Wright, with unbounded generosity, sent me digital photographs of its pages. I began to explore the internet. One Google search took me aback. I opened the page of www.robbenislandbibleblogspot.com and was surprised to find myself reading the opening paragraphs of my inaugural lecture. The blog belongs to Matthew Hahn, a theatre practitioner and teacher at St Mary's University College, London, who has done more than anyone else to celebrate, extend and preserve the existence of the Robben Island Shakespeare (or, as he calls it, the Robben Island Bible). Matthew travelled to South Africa, tracking the 'bible' and its protagonists, interviewing them, making them his friends and forging from the Shakespeare text and the history of its signatories a remarkable play and a blog recording his experiences and activities:

> In July of 2011 I was asked to sign copies of my play, *The Robben Island Bible*, to be among the gifts presented by David Cameron to Nelson Mandela for his 93rd birthday. A further copy was presented by the Prime Minister to Archbishop Desmond Tutu.
>
> My play involves interviewing former political prisoners of Robben Island in Cape Town, South Africa who had annotated a smuggled copy of the Complete Works of Shakespeare. Disguised as a religious text in order to deceive the guards, the book became known as the 'Robben Island Bible' and was passed from prisoner to prisoner each of whom marked passages of particular significance to their own lives.
>
> This verbatim play is based [*sic*] these selected texts and on interviews with a number of these ex-political prisoners who survived the harsh regime of the prison and the system of apartheid.
>
> It was a great honour for my play to be chosen as a gift for Nelson Mandela. I interviewed the most gentle of men and their stories had a profound effect on me.

Without Matthew's dedication, support and unstinting generosity, this book would be a much smaller thing. He has given me access to all the interviews he conducted with the ex-prisoners, allowed me to quote from them, sent me iterations of his wonderful play and engaged in conversations and offered advice critical about the extraordinary series of events and texts that each of us, in very different ways, seeks to celebrate.

Parts of Chapter 2 have appeared in a different form in 'Hamlet's dreams', *Social Dynamics* 32.1 (2006), 1–21 and 'Chronotopes of the self in the writings of women political prisoners in South Africa', in *Apartheid Narratives*, ed. Nahem Yousaf (Amsterdam and New York: Rodopi, 2001).

I wish to thank colleagues and friends for encouragement, suggestions and critical comments along the long trajectory of this project: Jerry Brotton, Braden Cormack, Natasha Distiller, Colette Gordon, John Higgins, Christina Murray, Jonathan Lear, Michael Neill, David Nirenberg, Daniel Roux, Richard Strier, Gail Kern Paster, Christopher Thurman, Stanley Wells, Lesley Witz; the editors of *Shakespeare Now*, Simon Palfrey and Ewan Fernie; and the Arden editor, Margaret Bartley, without whose encouragement, guidance and support this book would not have been written. I also owe an immense debt to Lawrence Wright, who sent me his photographs of the pages of the Robben Island Shakespeare.

A few weeks before I was about to deliver the manuscript of this book to my editors I experienced the nightmare that haunts all scholars. A colleague in South Africa, Christopher Thurman, informed me of the very recent publication of a book called *Reading Revolution: Shakespeare on Robben Island*, by Ashwin Desai, Director of the Centre for Sociological Research at the University of South Africa.[4] Chris sent me a copy. Desai's book

[4] Desai, *Reading Revolution*.

is a compelling overview of the role of reading and education in the experience of Robben Island prisoners, complete with many illustrations and interviews with some of the people who signed the Robben Island Shakespeare. Shakespeare plays a large, but not overwhelming, role in his discussion. We necessarily travel some of the same paths, but we diverge in analytical perspective, personal narrative and overall direction of our arguments. Many of his interviews underscore my impressions and those obtained by Hahn; inevitably, Desai and I end with the question of South Africa's future and how Robben Island contributed to its shape and direction. Since this book has space for very few illustrations, I'm delighted that its readers can now see, at least in part, the pages of the Robben Island Shakespeare and other supporting pictures in *Reading Revolution* and get an alternative perspective on this remarkable text.

Introduction:
Home and Away

My first encounter with Shakespeare happened in the cramped space between my father's chair and the bookshelf under the window-seat behind it – under the casement that looked out through the frangipani tree, across the desiccated lawn and rock garden up onto the kopje where, 10 years later, I would shoot *dassies* – rock hyraxes to the rest of the world, and the closest relative to the elephant – with my Anschutz Match .22 target rifle. (They ate my mother's gladiolus bulbs.) Besides, it was thrilling to be able to co-ordinate hand, eye, and German precision engineering in a split-second of focused concentration, to the point at which the bundle of brown fur would drop from the rock 200 yards up the slope of the hill, to a mixture of elation and nagging guilt.

My father belonged to a book club that mailed him a book a month in gloriously impressive embossed faux leather and gold lettering. There were no bookshops within 70 miles of our house, so he ordered his reading from Johannesburg, 250 miles along the railway line and its accompanying tarred road to the north. The volumes under the window were lined in satisfying rows – uniform but for their slight variation in thickness and title. They bore intriguing names like Desmond Bagley and Hammond Innes and Alistair McLean and Georgette Heyer; their even ranks grew each month by one more title. But one book stood out from the rest. Dark blue, with a soft, matt cover and glorious gold on the outer edges of its pages, it drew attention to itself for other reasons – its difference in size and thickness; the alien distribution of its faint blue words across the pages, made up mostly of names and short, staggering lines; but most of all for the exotic world of its pictures: strange configurations of young men in bright clothes and pretty but slightly disfigured women, older men in cloaks and crowns and wild beards; others in armour with swords and horses; and, most absorbing, scenes with wild seas and storms and shipwrecks and misshapen monster figures: witches and ghosts and dark malignant figures in wind-swept coats with strangely angular features.

I spent hours absorbed by these pictures, returning to them again and again in the small space on the floor, even though I had to contort my small body to extract the book and then lie on the cool, smooth wood of the floor to gaze at its pages in the pale winter sun that poured through the window. Once I asked my mother, who was knitting nearby, what the book was. 'Nothing', she replied evasively, if not exactly dismissively. 'Just a book of dad's. It's not for you.' I had never seen my father reading it, so I was puzzled, if not put off entirely. I would return to my space behind the chair, to gaze at the pictures, and occasionally try to read a couple of lines of its strange language, equally opaque and evocative of a world I could sense only very dimly, as if in a dream.

I grew up on a rural diamond mine in the Orange Free State – an amalgamation of the corn and bible belts of the United States – in a South Africa for which Apartheid had seemed the most natural thing in the world, ordained by God, ingrained into the landscape and the sun and the very air we breathed, uncontested by the books we were allowed to read and possess and the radio we listened to every night. (There was no TV; it was in the view of the Calvinist Minister of Posts and Telegraphs, the 'instrument of the devil'.) As children, we lived the inevitability of apartheid in our relations with the servants who tended to our immediate needs, and the labourers confined in the compounds enclosed within the mine. My father was the manager of this small mine owned by Goldfields, one of the leading international mining companies, with its head office in London, a city as heady, strange and enchanting and distant to me as the volume of Shakespeare behind my father's chair.

Until I was nine I attended the local farm school: two pre-fabricated buildings divided into three classrooms, shaded by bluegum trees, and surrounded by the green and gold of maize fields, to which we were ferried in the mine dynamite truck, its red flags removed for human cargo. The girls from the surrounding farms would be dropped by horse and buggy, while the older, tougher farm boys, barefoot and in khaki shorts, rode their horses to school. The school divided us into two groups: grades one to four in one classroom; grades five and six and seven in another. The latter were taught simultaneously, by the headmaster, *Meneer* Lindeque. He would walk, tall and stooped, with his balding head and wispy grey hair, across the flinty playground from his house, always clutching a black book in his gnarled, arthritic hands. We did not read Shakespeare, but I did find a clutch of English fairytales in a dusty cupboard in the empty classroom, whose pictures and stories entranced me almost as much as the strange blue volume at home. The headmaster occasionally allowed me to teach my friends and fellow students, all of them Afrikaans-speaking, how to read and write English when he was busy with another grade – although we once disagreed violently about whether 'got' (which I taught to the unsuspecting children) was bad English. He insisted that it was ungrammatical and uncultivated. I insisted, at the age of seven, like one of Shakespeare's smart-alec kids, that I was right: he was after all Afrikaans, like my father; but my mother had been born in Scotland, and we said 'got' all the time at home.

Home: the concept has very little secure place in Shakespeare, all of whose plays, comedy and history, tragedy and late, are steeped in its fundamental strangeness and its continuous, often violent, displacement. Think of the early comedies, *The Comedy of Errors* and *The Two Gentlemen of Verona*, which establish the fundamental motifs of alienation, loss and displaced recovery in *A Midsummer Night's Dream* and *Twelfth Night*, and which become the driving concerns of the late plays, *Pericles*, *Cymbeline*, *The Winter's Tale* and *The Tempest*. In the histories home is always contested, split between

Lancaster and York or England and France. And in the tragedies home itself is revealed to be *Heimlich* in the Freudian sense of the word, which is to say *unheimlich*: strange, alien, uncanny, a place of violence and self-destruction. The Macbeths turn their home and country into a slaughter-house; Lear dismembers his country and family only to cast himself out into the wilderness; Othello finds in his new home the horror of his own self-betrayal and blind violence; Romeo and Juliet discover that love for each other places them in a world where the only home is the grave; Antony is torn between Rome and Egypt; Coriolanus declares of his home, 'there is a world elsewhere'; and Hamlet returns home from the university to find a prison.

At the age of nine I was sent away from home to what seemed a prison, an Anglican Church[1] boarding-school 70 miles away in Bloemfontein, for a 'proper' education. It was a miserable place – mean, violent, beset by the petty but constant miseries of cold and hunger, bullying and what passes for community life among pre-adolescent and adolescent boys and warped men. It was run along lines that Foucault perceptively found in all the repressive institutions of modernity: it disciplined the soul by provoking a continuous state of fear and anxiety through the threat of continuous surveillance. One's condition was always that of a yet-undiscovered criminal: who had walked on the lawn reserved for the prefect class, or put his hands in his pockets, or left his blazer unbuttoned or laughed while singing a hymn in the chapel out of the sheer joy of being able to do something wholeheartedly unconstrained.[2] The order for Morning Prayer from the *1559 Book of Common Prayer* encapsulated the monotonous state of anxiety of our daily existence (and, presumably, Shakespeare's 400 years earlier): 'We have left undone those things which we ought to have done, and we have done those things which we ought not to have done, and there is no health in us. . . .'

It was also a place of Shakespeare, distributed between the relative enchantment of school theatre and grind of the classroom. I was especially impressed in my first year there, at the age of nine, by a production of *Twelfth Night* – my first encounter with the theatre – of which I now remember two things: the absolute magic of the purple cyclorama behind the cross-gartered figure of Malvolio, and Fabian's exotic warning to Aguecheek, 'you are now sailed into the north of my lady's opinion, where you will hang like an icicle on a Dutchman's beard unless you do redeem it by some laudable attempt either of valour or policy' (3.2.23–7). I don't know why I found that line so memorable; perhaps because my Afrikaans name sometimes brought upon me the gentle insult of 'Dutchman' from the English-speaking boys.

It was on the diamond mine, during the holidays at home, however, that Shakespeare took shape for me. My best friend had a Hungarian mother who was much better educated than everyone else, certainly than her sinewy Welsh husband, Taffy. I harboured a secret fantasy that she was a countess who had had to flee the Nazis; and who is to say that I was wrong? The point is, she *read*, and she encouraged her son and me to read. Most important, she had all the Shakespeare tragedies on long-playing records read by members of the Marlowe Dramatic Society. So Ian Holme, Michael Redgrave and Peggy Ashcroft filled the alien air with the sounds of Shakespeare while, 12-year-olds home for the holidays, we sat gazing at the inner sleeves in red and blue and yellow, each a silhouette of Shakespeare, feeling very grown-up and somehow above our African surroundings.[3]

If I were asked when I first heard of Robben Island or Nelson Mandela I would be unable to say. This is disgraceful. Not because they were a part of the fabric of life that one absorbed without noticing it. I don't know, but I doubt it. Nor because I can't put an exact hour or day or even year to my first knowledge of these absolute landmarks of South African twentieth-century history. It is rather that in acquiring knowledge of them, as a white boy growing up in the rural hinterland of apartheid, they simply made no mark. We all liked to think of ourselves as being violently against the Nationalist regime and their segregationist policies, and we debated politics earnestly in the debating society and the current affairs club. But I was perfectly happy to work on the mine my father managed for the London capitalists for my university allowance, even though it combined the exploitative indifference of capital with the harshest of apartheid's laws. Not only were the most menial jobs reserved by the country's laws for blacks but the mine's owners and shareholders were also allowed to force black workers to remain within a small, barbed-wired compound for a full year. They lived in crowded dormitories, hemmed in by wire and guards, and worked long, 12-hour days for a pittance. For most of them it was an endlessly recurring, one-year sentence, reiterated through what was complacently thought of as the freedom of contract. I was working to buy a car and keep my girlfriend happy in steakhouses; the men who worked underground were eking out a living for their families thousands of miles away. Reason not the need!

It could be argued in mitigation of my failure of memory that the regime had done everything in its power to obliterate the name of Mandela and his comrades. Everything he had written or said was banned; so was any photograph or image of him. The massacre at Sharpville in 1961, which proved a symbolic turning point in the resistance, occurred when I was six; Mandela's Rivonia trial, another landmark, which sent him to prison on Robben Island in 1964, when I was ten; he was released in 1990, when I was 35.

Shadows

In 1973, the United Nations General Assembly adopted the International Convention on the Suppression and Punishment of the Crime of Apartheid.[4] This resolution declared Apartheid a crime, and called upon the South African Government to release everyone 'imprisoned, interned, or otherwise restricted' for opposing Apartheid. In South Africa that year also saw the beginning of major labour unrest in Durban and the initial deployment of units of the South African Police to Namibia (then South West Africa) to counter an insurgency by the South West African People's Organization (Swapo). Internationally, the most significant event of the year 1973 was the Yom Kippur war between Israel and her Arab neighbours.

In 1973, I was in my second year at the University of Stellenbosch, then the intellectual home of the Afrikaner: it was the Oxbridge of Afrikaans culture – the university that had produced all South African Prime Ministers except one, P. W. Botha. In the words of the Nationalist politician who instituted the policy of racial separation as Prime Minister in 1948, Dr D. F. Malan, 'Stellenbosch represents an idea'. That inaugurating idea was the *idee fixe* of the Afrikaner Nation and its destiny as a superior race apart. I had gone to Stellenbosch because I wanted to study law; its Law Faculty was considered by many to be the best in the country, and I felt a nagging duty to my Afrikaans father to return to the paterfamilias roots. I soon tired of what appeared to me as the arcane rigours and dry positivism of the Law. I was seduced instead by Philosophy, English Literature and the stage. In 1973, I was switching to majors in English Literature and Political Philosophy, both with a local reputation for their internally subversive resistance to Apartheid and the ethos of its intellectual home, although the intensely Leavisite English department held the liberal-humanist line that literature transcended the political in favour of the universally human. It also stuck resolutely to its beliefs that all but one or two texts from Africa (those espousing liberal humanism in South Africa, of course) did not make the grade as literature. Shakespeare and Chaucer were the gold standards of literary excellence, followed by the novels singled out in *The Great Tradition*, and the generally recognized poets from the Metaphysicals to Wordsworth, Yeats, T. S. Eliot and, ultimately, W. H. Auden. (Auden died in 1973.)

I also threw myself wholeheartedly into the student dramatic society. I acted the parts of the King in *Henry IV, Part I*, Pompey in

*Measure for Measure*and Lysander in *A Midsummer Night's Dream*, and felt all the resentment of which an inflated undergraduate is capable at being given a very poor mark for an essay that argued that Falstaff is essentially corrupt and needed to be banished by the new King Henry V when, as someone who had actually acted in the play, I knew better. (I will return to Falstaff in Chapter 3.) There were sporadic and half-hearted protests by a handful of Stellenbosch students against the regime, which led to the comment by the then Prime Minister and Chancellor of the university, B. J. Vorster, that it harboured 'spineless Afrikaners'. I was approached by one of these Afrikaners whose backbone had deserted him, an already lauded Afrikaans poet and son of the Vice-Chancellor of one of the Apartheid universities reserved only for people of Asian and Indian extraction, to take part in a small, experimental protest in downtown Cape Town. We were to do some 'street theatre': at midday a troupe of clowns would occupy some space in one of the city squares, silently tumbling and juggling. When a crowd had gathered (contrary to the laws of assembly at the time), one of us would appear with a loudhailer, tell the crowd that they were gathered illegally, order them to disperse, 'arrest' the clowns and we would all depart in a car that was scheduled to appear at the appointed time. Since my talents extended to neither tumbling nor juggling, I was cast in the role of the 'security policemen' – the only speaking part in the 15-minute traffic of our stage.

It seemed simple enough – even quite exciting and daring. I agreed, assuming that it would all fall pat as they told me. I dressed in a dark suit, trimmed my beard, the clowns tumbled into the car and we set off on the 45-minute trip to the city. It went as expected: the clowns did their impromptu things, a sizable crowd did gather, and on cue I stepped forward, announcing to the assembly in English and Afrikaans that they should disassemble. At no point did I represent myself as a policeman. I simply acted as I thought one would act. What I didn't expect was any resistance from the crowd. As soon as I had completed my announcement, a mild-looking, bespectacled man with a grey beard asked me, in heavily accented Afrikaans, who I was to have assumed the authority to ask them to leave. I had not anticipated such a challenge. I recall the shock of this confrontation as a sudden change in my perception of my own body and its circumstances. My stomach tightened, I felt a constriction about my chest and a dryness in my mouth. 'Who are you to ask me who I am?' I asked in Afrikaans, slowly and menacingly, struggling to keep myself under control. He persisted with his initial question. I began to panic. I knew that whatever I did I could not represent myself explicitly as a police officer, but I was getting angry, overcome by a cold fury towards this obstreperous, impertinent man some thirty years my senior. We were face to face, barely a foot apart, now the objects of rapt attention by a larger crowd. *Where is that bloody car . . .?* I felt a tension between terror, on the one hand, at being no more than a student doing something mildly daring that was moving beyond my control, and the increasing weight of the role that was now playing me. I was overtaken by a general fury and sense of egotistical power: how dare this man cross me, how dare this stupid crowd stand there with their smirks and smiles? I began to threaten the man, my voice rising, my body quivering. *Where IS that BLOODY car?* At the point at which I felt I might drive my fist into my challenger's face, the car arrived with a squeal of tires. With a parting threat I turned to round up my companions. The clowns, sensing the opportunity for more fun, began to run away, dodging through the crowd, using them as barriers and (so I imagined) taunting me. I caught one by the sleeve, and pulling him violently towards me, swung my fist at him, missing his face and merely brushing his shoulder. I felt hands steering me, pushing me into the car, a door slammed and we were racing away. I began to shiver and sob without control.

It took a great deal to persuade me to repeat the performance the following day, in a different square. The event went off without incident. I encountered no difficult bystander; the car arrived on time; the crowd seemed mildly bemused by the whole affair.

I heard subsequently that members of the security police had arrived at the university drama department with photographs of me and my loudhailer, asking the university authorities to identify me. If these stories are to be believed, I presume that since I was a Philosophy and English major and not a Drama student, the Drama Department had no idea who I was, and the police left none the wiser.

I was acting in a production of *A Midsummer Night's Dream* at the time, and I thought whimsically that if I were to be arrested by the police, I could try Puck's excuse:

> If we shadows have offended,
> Think but this, and all is mended,
> That you have but slumber'd here
> While these visions did appear.
> And this weak and idle theme,
> No more yielding but a dream.
>
> (*A Midsummer Night's Dream*, Epilogue, 1–6)

I wonder how they would have responded. I indulged myself with the thought that I might have persuaded them to consider Theseus's indulgent patronage: 'The best in this kind are but shadows, and the worst are no worse if imagination amend them' (5.1.210–11).

Despite my act of mildly daring insubordination, the shadows, for me and for almost all white South Africans, were the prisoners on the Island, no more than five miles away from the squares in which we had staged our performances, confined by concrete, steel, a narrow, cold icy sea, and the regime's propaganda machine to a suffering, liminal purgatory.[5]

* * *

The conjunction of Shakespeare and the South African prison at an exhibition in England in 2006 fortuitously brought together two things that I have worked on – albeit quite separately. In the mid-1980s, when I was a lecturer at the Rand Afrikaans University in

Johannesburg, I came across Breyten Breytenbach's *True Confessions of an Albino Terrorist* – his memoir of his own capture, interrogation, trial and imprisonment under the Terrorism Act. Breytenbach, who was in the peculiar position of simultaneously being Afrikanerdom's most celebrated living poet and its most reviled traitor, opened a world for me that in 1986, in the midst of the most intense forms of unrest and repressive reaction in South Africa, was still difficult to access, both in real and literary terms. Most memoirs by political prisoners, both black and white, were banned, some for possession. Press censorship was such that the left-wing newspaper, *The Weekly Mail*, regularly appeared with much of its copy blacked out (like the 500-word letters that political prisoners were permitted to send and receive from members of their family). Four years later, the ANC, South African Communist Party and the Pan African Congress (PAC) – the mere membership of which could have lead to detention – became free political parties. Nelson Mandela was released, and in due course, all political prisoners. South Africans began a process of negotiation that led to free elections and a non-racial democracy.

What role did Shakespeare play in this process? In his pioneering study, *Shakespeare Against Apartheid*, Martin Orkin castigated white, liberal, English-speaking academics and teachers for perpetuating a strangely paradoxical liberal-humanist Shakespeare who, by remaining above politics, had been mobilized as part of the neo-colonialist racism of the Apartheid regime.[6] David Johnson's *Shakespeare in South Africa* was no more optimistic.[7] He saw even in the engagement of native South Africans such as Sol T. Plaatje with Shakespeare abject collaboration with the twinned forces of capital and racial and cultural chauvinism. Responding to both these writers, Natasha Distiller paid careful attention to local contexts and histories of the much-derided role precisely of humanism, and to a lesser degree, liberalism, in shaping opposition to apartheid and the subjectivities of a number of local writers who made Shakespeare their own in the first half of the twentieth century. She includes Sol Plaatje, but also discusses significant black writers of the

1950s – Peter Abrahams, Can Themba and Blake Modisane – who were active at precisely the moment when Nelson Mandela and his companions were forging resistance to apartheid in the shantytowns of Johannesburg. Distiller reminds us that these figures internalized and mobilized the multivalent differences that are collected under the proper name, 'William Shakespeare', in service of a specifically South African, black identity.[8]

Lewis Nkosi writes, somewhat romantically, perhaps, of an Elizabethan tenor to the simultaneously dangerous and flamboyant world of township gangsters and late-night dives:

> It was the cacophonous, swaggering world of Elizabethan England, which gave us the closest parallel to our own mode of existence; the cloak and dagger stories of Shakespeare; the marvelously gay and dangerous time of change . . . reflecting our own condition. Thus it was possible for an African musician returning home at night to inspire awe in the group of thugs surrounding him by declaiming in an impossibly archaic English: 'Unhand me, rogues!' Indeed they did unhand him. The same thugs . . . also delighted in the violent colour, the rolling rhetoric of Shakespearean theatre. Their favourite form of persecuting middle-class Africans was forcing them to stand at street corners, reciting some passage from Shakespeare, for which they would be showered with sincere applause.[9]

Nelson Mandela famously recalled the lines from *Measure for Measure*, 'Be absolute for death, either life or death / Shall thereby be the sweeter' on the eve of his sentencing during the Rivonia trial, when the death penalty was a strong possibility.[10] And Mandela's rival and comrade, leader of the PAC, Robert Sobukwe (who was kept in solitary confinement on Robben Island for part of the time that Mandela was there), had before his imprisonment embarked on a translation of *Macbeth* into Zulu as part of a project to translate all of Shakespeare's plays into his native language 'to demonstrate the power and the beauty of the Zulu language, and because of the power of the original English'.[11]

Anders Hallengren observes that, 'Unlike the Bible, the *Quran*, the *Bhagavadgita*, or *Das Kapital* by Karl Marx, Shakespeare was a common denominator for the prisoners at Robben Island. Only a few of them were Christian believers; a few were Moslems or Hindus; a few, communists; and their origins were different. They all knew Shakespeare, however'.[12] Sampson echoes this claim: 'if the Robben islanders had a common culture and text, it was not the Bible, or the Koran, but Shakespeare',[13] and the sentiment is re-echoed in Tom Lodge's much later biography: 'Many of the prisoners found ways of universalizing their experience through their reading'; Shakespeare provided a 'common text'.[14]

These are difficult claims to evaluate, especially as a Shakespearean averse to the exaggeration of Shakespeare's influence or importance. In the light of the fact that the Robben Island Shakespeare circulated among no more than 34 of the isolated, B-section's prisoners, and that many of the thousands of other prisoners in the general sections were illiterate, Hallengren's proposal not only that everybody knew Shakespeare but also that he acted as a universal bonding agent, is a wild exaggeration. (He does not say that everyone knew *of* Shakespeare – which would itself be contestable.) Lodge's more carefully qualified assertion is probably closer to the truth.

In her introduction to her essay, 'Reading Debating/Debating Reading: The Case of the Lovedale Literary Society, or Why Mandela Quotes Shakespeare', Isabel Hofmeyr notes that 'as many commentators have noted, Nelson Mandela has a proclivity for quoting Shakespeare', and then lists a number of speeches in which Shakespeare is included.[15] Mandela may well have an abiding love for Shakespeare, but the President's speeches are usually the work of speech-writers, who may be reflecting public expectations, their own inclinations or the general culture of Shakespeare as a necessary part of the political speech, rather than any proclivity of the politician themselves. Hofmeyr in fact goes on to show that there is indeed no easy answer as to why Mandela quotes Shakespeare. She argues that in the mission schools like Lovedale, where a number of the African elite were educated, the concept of 'literature' was contested, its role and purpose divided between the traditional view of the teachers that it should be a civilizing and moral influence and the increasingly activist view of the students that it is grist to the mill of the broader activity of 'debating'. The formal qualities of the debate allowed for the discussion of pressing political and cultural issues as part of the development of the skills required for *leadership*: 'Under student leadership, the proportion of debates went up, and the degree of literary talks declined . . . Their views of literature were subordinated to this prerogative, and literature became a resource to buttress this political prerogative' (Hofmeyr, 266, 269). What was true of Lovedale could be applied to the Robben Island Prison, where the gathering impulse was to turn the prison into a resource for political leadership through education and debate and where literature tended to be viewed as an instrument for that purpose.

It is clear that those who made their personal marks of identification in Venkatrathnam's book found something in Shakespeare – whether from their time at school, or before they entered the prison, or even in the prison itself, through which they could express their personal and collective voices. If Shakespeare may be said to have invigorated the bleak life of the Robben Island elite, Robben Island itself also invigorated and legitimized the idea of Shakespeare in that exhibition in his hometown. Having been circulated stealthily as a force of memory, inspiration, perhaps even of mere piety in the South African prison more than two decades ago, Shakespeare was himself released (like Prospero) in a contemporary British exhibition by the mythical force of Mandela and his island. As I write, the Robben Island Shakespeare is a major exhibit in the London 2012 Olympics exhibition, 'Shakespeare, Staging the World', at the British Museum, and is the subject of much, often inflated and misguided, media attention.[16]

Ahmed Kathrada, one of the Robben Island Shakespeare's signatories, and a self-confessed lover of the Bard, who had his own copy of the Works on the Island, invokes Shakespeare on four occasions in his *Letters from Robben Island*, stating as early as his first letter that he 'still recites the passages from Shakespeare daily, which brings back a host of pleasant and cherished memories'.[17] But in his later memoir, *No Bread for Mandela*, he mentions Shostakovitch but *not* Shakespeare. At first sight, it is strange that the published selection from his prison notebooks that record memorable quotations from literary texts includes Donne and Herbert, Euripides and Sophocles, Lewis Carrol and Charles Chaplin, but not the Bard of Stratford. Matthew Hahn, however, tells me that Kathrada has told him that he deliberately excluded Shakespeare because 'there was just too much'.[18] Nevertheless, it is striking that Kathrada finds a quotation from Chaplin's *My Autobiography* that records the actor's aversion to Shakespeare striking enough to include it:

> I dislike Shakespearean themes involving Kings, Queens, august people and their honour. In my pursuit of bread and cheese, honour was seldom trafficked in. I cannot identify with a prince's problems. Hamlet's mother could have slept with everyone at court and I would still be indifferent to the hurt it would have inflicted on Hamlet.[19]

It is safe to say that Chaplin's indifference to Shakespeare is echoed in the *general* absence of the dramatist from the memorialized life of the island. If the memoirs are to be trusted, he appears at best to have been a marginal figure for most of them, invoked or discussed occasionally or in order to meet an expectation of cultural literacy.[20] None of the signatories of the Shakespeare text who subsequently wrote of their time on the island – Mandela, Michael Dingake, Eddie Daniels or even Kathrada – mentions the book or their signing of it in their memoirs.[21] Indeed, if anything was absolutely central to the prisoners it was news – signalled in the absolutely obessive, reiterated desire for magazines and newspapers, rather than Shakespeare or Dickens.

That said, we need to account for the fact that, once prisoners were permitted to have their own books on the island and share them, some did have copies of Shakespeare. Neville Alexander mentions his copy. But, unlike Venkatrathnam and Kathrada, he left it behind when he was released. In recent interviews that specifically ask about Shakespeare on the island, we are beginning to hear of performances of *Coriolanus*, *Richard III* and *Antony and Cleopatra*.[22] We may assume, then, that interest in Shakespeare was distributed unevenly among the prisoners. Some, like Kathrada, found in Shakespeare a source of vitality, reflection, creativity and personal identity (but that did not prevent him from omitting Shakespeare from his own memoir and Mandela's autobiography, on which he collaborated). Others would have known and enjoyed Shakespeare, but as a relatively marginal figure, while yet others might have encountered him in passing as part of their university or school syllabus.

Marcus Solomon, actively involved in the educational project on the Island, remarks:

> I think Shakespeare was important at that time because his writings covered such a wide range of experiences and emotions . . . we could read what suited us and fitted in with our moods at any particular time. What made him accessible to many inmates was that almost anyone who was studying what was then called standard six or higher had read him as part of their prescribed reading. So many inmates, to different degrees, had knowledge of his writing . . . It is not unimportant that Shakespeare can be quoted to fit almost any situation, so chaps liked to quote him. (Desai, *Reading Revolution*, 58)

This comment underscores Hofmeyr's point that literature in the context of the growing politicization of missionary school students becomes an extension of 'debate', and what Shakespeare has to offer is not a resistant representation of a set of politically and culturally charged human encounters and problems, but a pliant sounding-board to be read for the ways in which he could fit specific 'moods' and 'particular situations'. This can sometimes lead to the most banal reduction of Shakespeare to an instrument of hackneyed or folk platitude, as when Desai claims that Mzwandile Mdingi's love for Macbeth's 'Out, out brief candle! / Life's but a walking shadow' (*Macbeth,* 5.5.23–4) 'signified that life is short and that a revolutionary must hasten to act if he wants to see change in his lifetime' (Desai, 33). It also shows that Shakespeare was not always read for the dialogical complexity of situated interaction, but rather cherry picked for isolated instances of folk wisdom. This tendency is exemplified by Michael Dinkake's choice of Polonius's self-important advice to his son Laertes. Most Shakespeare critics and scholars would cringe at the seriousness with which the father's 'few precepts' (1.3.58) are 'character'd' 'in [the] memory' of the play's Robben Island readers. But such a response overlooks the frank appeal of Polonius's advice as a recipe for practical life. 'Be thou familiar but, but by no means vulgar . . . neither a borrower nor a lender be . . . Give every man thy voice, but few thine ear . . . those friends thou hast, and their adoption tried / Grapple them to thy soul with hoops of steel' and 'to thy own self be true' (1.3.55–80) – who could possibly take exception to these bits of practical advice from father to son?

Many of the passages marked by the prisoners, I suspect, resulted from a prior 'commonplacing' of striking expressions rather than a fresh appreciation of the complete play read within the new context of the prison.[23] Otherwise, how could Dingake, a strikingly informed and intelligent commentator on his situation, have missed Shakespeare's canny placing of a father's sage advice between that of a brother's hectoring attempts to control his sister's sexuality, on the one hand, and the father's engagement of a servant not only to spy on his son, but also to entrap him in questionable behaviour?

Viewed as an object *in fact* absent from the memories of Robben Island prisoners as they are presented in published memoirs or interviews *before* it became the object of intense scrutiny, enquiry and fascination, Shakespeare represented by Venkatrathnam's copy thus constitutes something of a blank: it is a repressed presence that has been forgotten, transformed, removed and now returned in unpredictable ways.[24] We know that at least 34 prisoners read it insofar as they marked it with the trace of their signatures. How they read it, why they read it, and in what spirit they did so is a mystery. Nor would it clarify that mystery to ask them. Matthew Hahn's interviews with some of the Robben Island Shakespeare's signatories for his play indicate that there is no easy path to the desires and motivations across two decades, an ocean, and a democratic revolution.

Here are three former prisoners, asked by Hahn to comment on their choices:

> *Ahmed Kathrada*: My trouble is, as I pointed out immediately, I just can't imagine myself having chosen that passage. I don't understand the passage. I don't know what to say about it. One has to read it in its context. I mean, I have got my Complete Works here which was with me on the island where I marked hundreds of passages – just things that I liked. This passage is not there. The passage made no impact on me. Years and years ago, I went through very hurriedly the Complete Works when I had nothing else to do, but there were passages that made an impact, which I can't off-hand remember. Some of them of course I do . . . Off-hand I remember, because I quoted it at the memorial service of Walter Sisulu, a former Robben Islander. I quoted that, 'His life was gentle; and the elements; So mixed in him, that Nature might stand up, And say to all the world, THIS WAS A MAN!'

> *Andrew Mlengeni*: I agree with what Kathrada is saying. We were ill prepared for this interview especially because I don't think that we were well informed as to what it is that you people want. What do you want us to do and so on and so forth. I said over

the telephone this morning, I just had no idea, I said, 'What is this "Robben Island Bible"'? What is it that people want to do? *The quotation mentioned there was not chosen by me.* Although somebody says that I marked it some years back. I don't know the reason for me for choosing that quotation. But the one that I do slightly, I was trying to look for it right now and I can't find it – the one quotation that I always liked was the one that says, 'uneasy lies the head that wears the crown'. And I understood that at that time, I don't know if my understanding was correct but if you are a king. . . . today you can talk of the President . . . of a country . . . but if you are a king, you, you, you, don't ever feel safe. You are always saying, 'Who's plotting to bring me down? Who's plotting against me?'

Kwede Mkalipi: Well, more or less I agree with my colleagues here. I am also not sure what we are coming here for. So, *because even this quote is not the quote that I had prepared myself.*[25]

These responses are complicated. Kathrada was right not to acknowledge the passage that Hahn showed him because Hahn had made a mistake in his identification of Kathrada's passage. But what Kathrada recalls as one that 'made an impact' is *not* Henry V's speech at Harfleur – the speech in the Shakespeare text that bears his name. It is rather Antony's encomium to Brutus in the final lines of *Julius Caesar*. This is perfectly understandable – the new context, in which he is called upon to speak at the funeral of a friend and comrade – will have given a completely different aspect of Shakespeare's text an immediate use value. Furthermore, Kathrada has very recently intervened in a significant way in the media claims about the significance of Venkatrathnam's copy of Shakespeare to the political struggle:

Ahmed Kathrada, who spent more than 26 years in prison – including 18 years on Robben Island alongside Mandela – also dismisses the [Robben Island Shakespeare] as unimportant.

> Kathrada said he couldn't remember Venkatrathnam or the passage he signed.
>
> 'He asked a number of us to sign our name beside the passage that you find interesting of Shakespeare. And that was the sum total of my connection', he told the *Star*. 'I have no other connection.'[26]

In the light of Kathrada's understandable failure to recognize the passage with which Hahn confronted him, it is difficult to explain Mlangeni and Mkalipi's refusal to acknowledge *their* passages. Hahn got these right. So, were they following Kathrada's cue, or would they independently have denied or forgotten the passages that they had indeed picked out 30 years earlier? In an interview with Hahn, Venkatrathnam himself draws attention to the suppression of memory and its roots in ideological changes in the beliefs, pursuits and lifestyles of many of his former comrades:

> Honestly I think, a lot of the people who chose particular lines very deliberately would today find it very difficult to identify themselves with that particular line or passage. Because, not only the political philosophy, and I always associated people's political philosophy with their own ideology and their vision of tomorrow. . . . So what I am saying is that . . . A lot of people that I thought would never change . . . ideologically . . . have switched horses. Yesterday's Communists are today's biggest Capitalists. I find that very difficult to reconcile. Very, very difficult . . . I'm not saying that they mustn't adapt and all of that, but to become so *virulently* Capitalist . . . that to me is, I don't think acceptable.[27]

This change from revolutionary prisoner to capitalist fat-cat is the subject of Chapter 3. For the moment I wish to note Venkatrathnam's sense that the choice of a passage from Shakespeare involves staking one's identity on that passage: it bears witness to a sense of self at a particular moment, and such a self-image is likely to change, sometimes in such a way that the signatory is prevented from recognizing himself in the mirror of Shakespeare's text.

Signatures

If Venkatrathnam's Shakespeare is part of a process of repression, forgetting and transformation, its inscriptions constitute a form of collective and individual unconscious. The book is a kind of 'common-place' book, popular in Shakespeare's own time, in which passages are marked for their special significance, poetic beauty, or moral weight. In more contemporary terms it is akin to a 'guest-book', in which visitors are asked to leave a mark of their presence at a particular moment. The passages marked by Mandela and his companions tell their own tales. Such tales are complicated, for they are told in the words of others. The words are in the strictest sense Shakespeare's; but they are also those of Shakespeare's imagined characters, who maintain an irreducible distance from their creator. However, each of the prisoners came to countersign Shakespeare's texts with their own names, they in some way recognized themselves, their desires, preoccupations or circumstances in those choices. What does it mean to sign one's name? What does it mean to mark the words of another with one's a name that is indubitably one's own?

A signature is the mark of the indubitable presence of the person who signs his (or her) name. But Jacques Derrida reminds us that it also belongs to the impersonal system of language, which, distancing the individual from the moment of presence, makes it possible for that moment to be archived.[28] The signature is simultaneously the sign of presence *and* absence. It is not only a singular event, a precise moment, an impression of presence but it is also a mark that divides itself through its necessary capacity to repeat itself differently at a different time from the present. When a signature pledges itself against a text written – and signed – by another

(Shakespeare) – it is redoubled. I sign my name at this moment against what is/was written by someone 400 years ago. In doing so, I mark these words with a part of myself. At the same time, I allow these words (which are also *those* words, since they are not mine) to make their (othering) mark upon me. I mark these words *as* part of myself. At this point, the presence that is the mark of the signature reveals itself as a sign of absence. For the signature's signal of the presence of myself as signatory is divided by what makes it possible: its capacity to be repeated, at different times and in different places. As a sign of my presence, it also enables forgetting, a loss of original memory. A signature that could not be repeated, and therefore be divided from itself, could not be what it is – the mark of a singular presence; a signature that could not be carried over to a new and therefore inevitably removed iteration could not enact itself as signature.

This complexity of the signature is redoubled in the case of the Robben Island Shakespeare. For there the signatory is signing himself against another name – 'Shakespeare' – and that name is multiplied in the names of the multiple characters who speak, both on their own behalf and in his name. Shakespeare is held hostage by the characters who appear in his name, and who therefore divide him from himself. Anyone who pledges himself against Shakespeare's characters thus gives himself up to being hostage both to the character and to Shakespeare – and to the accumulated other signatures that 'Shakespeare' has acquired over almost half a millennium. The depths of complexity here are almost dizzying – but they may be encompassed or, perhaps better, signaled by the notion of the unconscious, which suggests a difficult relation of simultaneous singularity and generality, agency and passivity, individuality and institutionality.

In an institution such as the prison, which is expressly designed to curtail agency to an absolute degree, the marking of the passages, the signing of one's name, and the inscription of the date, exemplify a free expression of selfhood. And yet, confronted with the evidence of that freedom and selfhood 30 years later, some of the signatories do not recognize the selves that they see in the mirror of Shakespeare's text. Some seek to deny those shadows. This underwrites the divided nature of the signature. For what Hahn's interviewees attest to under the signature of the interview is their failure to recognize their signatures, materially inscribed some three decades earlier on the pages of a book. The names are theirs; the peculiar singularity of the hand that inscribed the name is theirs; but the words that were marked by those hands are no longer recognized as being even remotely part of themselves. What is being denied are not Shakespeare's words so much as the moment of original engagement, in which a person at a specific moment recognized himself in the words of a stranger. What happens when the signatory does not recognize the self that speaks, dimly, from the signature? What might the shadow cast by the mark of the name say to us?

It is impossible to extrapolate from the signing of the passages from Shakespeare, in conjunction with general or specific accounts of experiences on the island, why these or those lines from Shakespeare might have made an impression on a person, in his isolated cell, at a specific moment within a decade or more of incarceration. Some may have chosen a passage because a single word or phrase glinted through the darkness; another might have chosen a speech that had seeped into the memory from school or been learnt off by heart; others may have read Shakespeare for the first time, and been struck by the way in which this or that play spoke to their personal condition or a broader social and political struggle. Others may have been moved by the way in which Shakespeare takes the reader away from the immediate pressures of existence – for the way in which the music of the words take flight beyond the presence of these walls, that gate, those fences. Others, like Toivo ja Toivo and Kadir Hassim, simply signed the book itself, as witness to a sense of solidarity unconnected with the meaning of this speech or that sonnet.

This project – to make some sense of the Robben Island Shakespeare and its signatures by making them available to the world – is beset by innumerable difficulties. It is an impossible task. But it is also irresistibly compelling. We have countless narratives – records of memory and memorialization – from and about Robben Island. Those stories are the outcomes of the unique combination of personal history, political conscience, and the peculiar hardships and possibilities for human companionship in an extremely localized space. In personal terms, the Robben Island Shakespeare is just one – perhaps minor – facet of those encounters. In Shakespearean terms, the signatures of those who signed the pages of the book place an indelible mark on Shakespeare himself – or who we take Shakespeare to be, and therefore upon the 'we' who claim to be Shakespeareans, and especially upon the 'I' who presumes to interpret these encounters. We have seen that what the signatories say or recall about the moment and the motivation of their signatures cannot be taken at face value. Three things, all in irreducible tension with each other, come together over this Shakespeare: the Shakespeare text, and all its multivalent significations and determinations; the signature with its peculiar, irreducible history; and the interpreter, for whom there is no Archimedean vantage-point, no 'view from nowhere'.

Given these difficulties, I am going to approach this unique text as a repository of collective and individual unconscious: a palimpsest or 'mystic writing pad' (as Freud calls it) through which each personal narrative that it has touched has been filtered and released, in words from a different world and time. Each speech has been countersigned by an inscription that speaks on behalf of that name, in that name, but without being, properly speaking, of that name. It is, after all, Shakespeare speaking in each instance, but it is Shakespeare as a mask of momentary self-recognition, a mirror of a particular soul in words that belong to and come from *another*. But Shakespeare does not speak for himself. In speaking for his text, and for and about those who signed it, *I* assumes an insupportable ethical burden.

Chapter 1

'This Island's Mine'

Most people know of Robben Island only as a political prison: the place where political prisoners, especially Nelson Mandela, were incarcerated for their opposition to the Apartheid regime between 1961 and 1991. 'The Island', as it is known among South Africans, is a flat, somewhat desolate outcrop of rock, sand and scrub some 8 miles or 12 km in the Atlantic Ocean off Cape Town. It lies virtually in the shadow of Table Mountain; its oblong form lies slightly closer to the western coast of Table Bay (Figure 1.1).

Figure 1.1 Rocky shore with view to Table Mountain.

Its closest analogue in Western history and mythology is San Francisco's Alacatraz: both are small, barren islands surrounded by treacherous currents that offer ideal locations for maximum security prisons. It differs from its American counterpart in having been used almost exclusively as a place of political banishment and incarceration. The Island has a much longer colonial history than the 30 years it served as an Apartheid prison, almost all of it as a purgatorial, liminal site of exile and punishment. Members of the indigenous population who resisted the occupation and rule of the early Dutch and subsequently the English settlers were confined to its bleak shores in the seventeenth and eighteenth centuries, while in the nineteenth and early twentieth centuries it was used as a repository for the mentally ill, sexually deviant and medical outcasts like lepers. As Harriet Deacon puts it, 'It is with the "low" . . . domains that Robben Island has most frequently been associated – with political opposition, insanity, criminality, dirt, disease, the poorer classes, the very bottom of Africa.'[1]

In 1948 the racialist National Party of South Africa won the general election on its election platform of Apartheid – an ideological distillation of white racial superiority and the separation of races that had informed colonial South Africa almost from the first settlement of Dutch colonists in 1652. The National Party government faced its first critical resistance from the African population on 21 March 1960, when, in a moment of both symbolic and real cataclysm, black protesters were fired upon by police at a township called Sharpville. Sixty-nine people were killed; 180 were wounded. This event, which received world attention, proved to be a turning point in modern South African history. The government declared a state of emergency; the black political organizations, the PAC, which had organized the protest, and the African National Congress (ANC), were banned; tens of thousands of political activists were detained.

Needing a secure place of detention for new detainees and convicted prisoners that it had transformed into political criminals, the Apartheid regime returned the desolate place of colonial exile and incarceration to its former purgatorial role of deportation and abuse.

Its first intake of political prisoners in 1961 consisted overwhelmingly of members of the PAC, a group that had split from the ANC in 1959 because it felt that the ANC was too racially inclusive, excessively open to Communist influence, and not properly focused on the oppression and ultimate liberation of Africans as such. In line with its general ideology of separation (thc litcral meaning of 'Apartheid'),[2] only male African, Indian and prisoners of mixed race ('Coloureds') were interned, after sentence by a court, on Robben Island. Black female political prisoners were consigned to Kroonstad Prison; white female political prisoners were kept at Barberton Prison; white male political prisoners at Pretoria Local Prison; and black political prisoners condemned to be hanged confined to death row in Pretoria Central Prison until their execution (Figure 1.2).

Figure 1.2 The entrance gate.

The earliest years were the harshest, with appalling acts of brutality by warders and almost intolerable conditions. Prisoners were forced to do backbreaking labour, subjected to a near-starvation diet and suffered intolerable cold in winter and heat in summer. The authorities also deliberately inserted common-law prisoners among the political recruits. They believed that the lack of political sensibility, the brutal self-interest and the gang-inflected terrorism of these convicts would both make life intolerable for the new political prisoners and act as disruptive spies and *agents provocateurs*. One of the early PAC prisoners describes the absolute otherness of these fellows in terms that reflect the racial stereotyping of his political opponents:

> I had never come across such a species of prisoners. My whole body trembled at the sight of them. Eyes lurking and blood-red, scars on their heads and faces, tattoos on their chests and arms, grim-faced, they looked at us [as] though they were going to devour us. We looked at them sympathetically. They were the products of apartheid justice. I wondered whether any of them would ever be rehabilitated to live normal lives again. It was only later that we heard about the havoc that some of them had done to some of our comrades – many of them belonged to the Big Fives, a prison gang that helped warders in ill-treating other prisoners.[3]

The most important prisoner on the island at this time was Robert Sobukwe, leader of the PAC, who, after the end of his sentence, was confined to a tiny cottage on the Island by a special act of Parliament. Sobukwe was held in solitary confinement for 6 years, in almost total isolation, but occasionally he was able to acknowledge the silent salute of work parties passing his cottage.

Nelson Mandela spent a brief period on the Island before he and others comprising the Rivonia group were sentenced to long terms of imprisonment, including life terms, on the Island in 1964.[4] Owing to the canny resistance of the political prisoners, conditions gradually improved, with a period of recidivist repression in the late sixties and early seventies.[5] The equilibrium of the political prisoners was disturbed in 1976, after a general uprising throughout the country led by young people, when a completely new generation, much more aggressively activist and defiant than the older one, entered the prison. Mandela and three of his fellow prisoners were transferred to Polsmoor Prison in the southern suburbs of Cape Town in 1982. All political prisoners left the Island in May 1991, and it was turned into a Museum. It is currently a World Heritage Site.[6]

Displacement and Repression

The longer history or memory of Robben Island has been displaced by its most recent past. It has become the signifier of what is in effect a very short period of its existence – the roughly 30 years that the Apartheid regime used it as the place to isolate and control black, male opponents of Apartheid. Furthermore, and perhaps not less inevitably, its general role as a political prison has been displaced by the signifier Nelson Mandela, whose overwhelming figure has tended to stand in for the island as a whole. A recent attempt by the Robben Island Museum to 'restore dignity for those who died during incarceration on Robben Island', for example, confines itself to the years between 1963 and 1990.[7] The outcasts – the sick, the insane, the deviant – of its earlier history remain forgotten and ignored, their loss of dignity forgotten, repressed or overlooked.

If Nelson Mandela has become a metonym for Robben Island, and if the very local experiences of its prisoners during a relatively brief period are in turn a metonym for the history of the Island as a whole, accounts of such experiences have themselves engaged in displacement and repression. Individual accounts of life as a prisoner on Robben Island undoubtedly confront the reader with a sickening and systematic regime of brutality, hardship and indignity. Many memoirs repeat landmark stories: the extreme brutality of warder Delport at the stone quarry and the reign of terror of the Kleynhans brothers – who buried a prisoner up to his neck in sand for a day and when he asked for water urinated in his mouth; the meanness and small-mindedness of successive commanding officers; the deprivations of censorship and the outlawing of all forms of news; the consistently bad food, ill-fitting clothes and the brutal cold, hunger and psychological deprivation of the punishment of solitary confinement.[8]

Counter to these stories runs a narrative of solidarity and comradeship – of the gradual political education of the common-law prisoners until they were removed; and of self-discovery and a grand project of universal education, so that by the time Mandela was released, Robben Island had become celebrated as 'the University', where a new, politically and generally literate citizenship for a liberated South Africa had been forged and internal differences overcome. Mandela's own widely read biography, *Long Walk to Freedom*, offers a peculiar perspective on the Island for a number of reasons: Mandela was isolated with some 30 or 40 prisoners considered to be leaders in a single-cell courtyard (section B) cut off from the general sections which contained thousands of men; he tended to be treated by the authorities with greater respect than other prisoners, and he was neither beaten nor tortured during his pretrial detention; and his autobiography was carefully crafted with a view to achieving reconciliation and a unified nation for the future that he inaugurated as the President of a democratic South Africa.

The representation of Robben Island as, ultimately, the ideologically unified possession of its prisoners has led to some scepticism about the memoirs as factual records of the actual conditions in the prison. Russell Ally, commenting at a seminar at the Institute for Advanced Social Research at the University of the Witwatersrand in 1994, observes:

> It was . . . difficult . . . to maintain my credulity. Now, far be it for me to call into question the fact that many people did come off the Island better educated, more politicized, more

> committed to the struggle, and so forth, but are there no stories of disillusionment? Was nobody's spirit broken on the Island? I ask this question not to belittle the experiences of any of the political prisoners . . . but rather to alert ourselves to the dangers of romanticising our history.[9]

Fran Buntman records a number of dissenting voices, including that of Saths Cooper (one of the Robben Island Shakespeare signatories), in her comprehensive and insightful *Robben Island and Prisoner Resistance to Apartheid*.[10] But perhaps the clearest indication of the problematic nature of the common story of unified resistance and universal personal growth is the fact that a number of interviews with Robben Island prisoners at the Mayibuye Centre at the University of the Western Cape (including some of Buntman's) are at the time of writing not freely accessible.

The full story of Robben Island is thus likely to remain relatively obscure. It is perhaps never recoverable, especially as the declared camaraderie begins to fracture in South Africa two decades after Mandela's release, and members of the present government who were held on Robben Island are perceived to be succumbing to corruption and self-enrichment at the expense of the people for whom the struggle was engaged.

There is thus no single 'Robben Island' – there are many, distributed across its differential history, on the one hand, and the various forms of experience of the prisoners who now call it their own, on the other. This differentiated experience stems from the variable conditions in the prison from its inception to the release of the last political inmate – as different prison regimes and commanding officers imposed changing forms of discipline (and indiscipline) in accordance with personal inclination or in response to events in South Africa and the world; as the prisoners themselves began to wrest some control and authority through their own forms of resistance; as conflicts and tensions from beyond the walls impacted upon the prison community itself; and in accordance with a differentiated treatment of different sectors of the prison – for example, the section B, single-cell prisoners like Mandela, the general C-section cell where study was permitted, and – until their removal – the gang-controlled terrain of the common-law prisoners. Desai records a telling interview with Marcus Solomon, who reports of his visit with his daughter to a model of Robben Island at the Mayibuye Centre at the University of the Western Cape:

> My daughter asked, daddy, where is your cell? I can't see this section because it was in the dark. The only light was in the single cells. In fact they've reduced Robben Island to the single cells. (Desai, *Reading Revolution*, 118)

Solomon's reference to a distanced 'they' who now make decisions about the Island indicates a clearly felt disjunction between Solomon as former prisoner and the new keepers of memory (Figure 1.3).

People tend to speak and write of Robben Island as a set of experiences that belongs to a single place and time and a coherent body of subjects, and Shakespeare's appeal to those subjects is often assumed to be more or less uniform. Two things stand out against this for my own narrative. First, the claim that Shakespeare constituted a 'common text' that united Robben Island's prisoners is a romantic notion imported from a world in which the Bard is simply assumed to play such a universalizing role everywhere. At best, the evidence from prison narratives suggests that if Shakespeare was central to the lives of individual prisoners such as Sonny Venkatrathnam and Ahmed Kathrada, he played little part in the stories that prisoners told of a regime of brutal oppression overcome through solidarity and an independent forging of an ideal community that was to be a model for a future South Africa. Second, whatever idealistic and noble purposes lay behind the forging of such a common narrative, that narrative involved the suppression, forgetting and repression of counter-narratives that may not have fitted the story of universal resistance, achieved community and mutual transcendence.

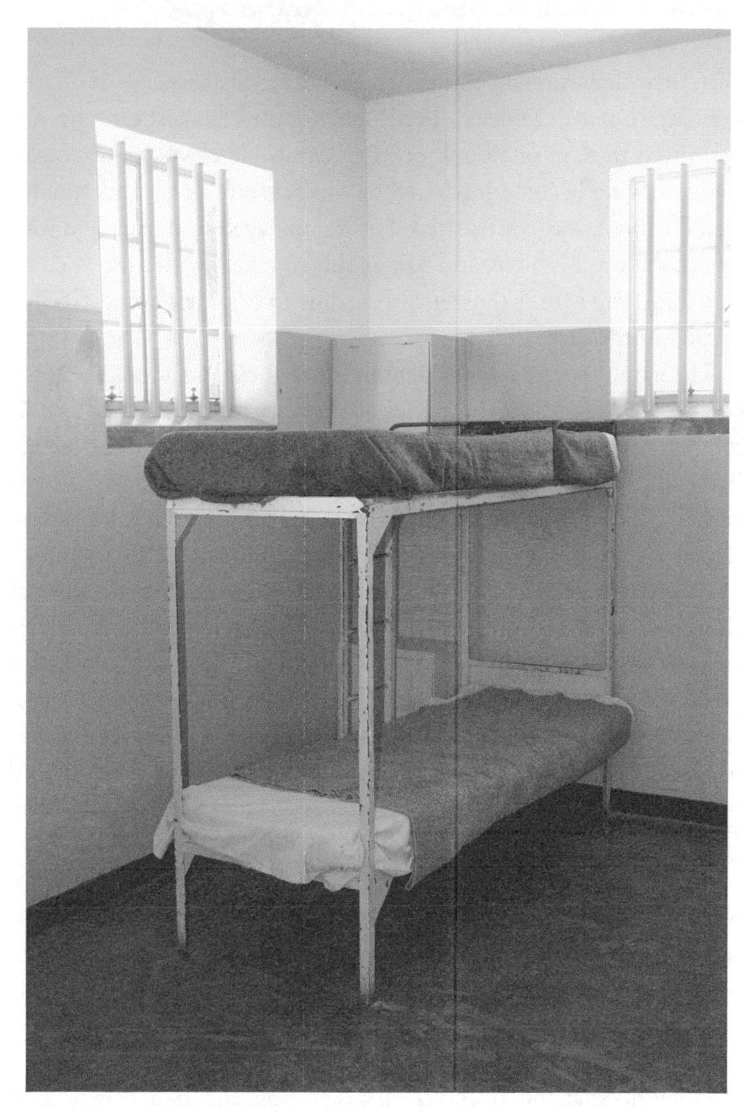

Figure 1.3 Bunk beds in a communal cell.

'Tomorrow and tomorrow and tomorrow'

The first signature on the Robben Island Shakespeare is 'S. K. Venkatrathnam'. Owner of the Robben island Shakespeare, he was permitted to have one book on the Island. He chose the *Complete Works*, having become intrigued by Shakespeare as an undergraduate. The book was confiscated, but he managed to persuade a warden that it was his bible, and so was able to take it with him when he was transferred from the general section to Mandela's single-cell B section in the early 1970s.

His name appears in confident italics that expand across the space on the title page below the names of Shakespeare and the book's editor, Peter Alexander. Beneath the signature, in caps, are three letters, 'RIP', and below that, the date, '9/5/72'.[11] Both the date and the indication of place (Robben Island Prison) suggest that Venkatrathnam signed his book shortly after he arrived on the Island. In the mode of the peculiar duplicity of all signatures, it thus does a number of things: it lays his claim to ownership of the physical book; it acts as a witness to the specificity of place and time; and it claims his affinity with the names above his. Others lay claim to particular passages; Venkatrathnam makes the whole Shakespeare text his own. Shakespeare, he says, 'has a very peculiar place in the hearts and minds of people. Shakespeare uniquely represents the universal man. It captures that essence' (Hahn interview and Desai, 13–14).

In subsequent interviews with prisoners the common notion of Shakespeare as representative and representer of all humanity is repeated with a kind of wonder and awe, especially by prisoners who went to the Island illiterate and who discovered Shakespeare in the prison.[12] Venkatrathnam was initially kept in the communal cells where, it appears, he told stories from Shakespeare to his fellows. He remarks that the 'peasants' in his section understood *King Lear* perfectly well, although they were puzzled that the king did not consult his elders about his actions – they would have put him right and prevented the suffering that ensued from them. Eddie Daniels says that his 'background is one of being illiterate' (Hahn interview, 3 February 2010). He left the Island with two university degrees from the correspondence University of South Africa, but had not heard of Shakespeare before he entered prison. He tells of playing the part of Marc Antony in *Julius Caesar* on the Island and declares that he 'loved *Macbeth*', in particular Macbeth's thoughts (which bear his signature in the book) upon the death of his wife: 'Tomorrow, and tomorrow and tomorrow creeps in this petty pace from day to day.' 'And that is our life', Daniels adds, poignantly, '"Tomorrow and tomorrow and tomorrow". And from babyhood you go through life, battling, struggling. Getting married. Getting degrees. Getting a big bank balance. And then we leave the earth as we came in, with nothing. With nothing. With nothing.'

Daniels internalizes and reiterates the rhetoric he so admires in Shakespeare, making the beating emptiness of nihilism in Macbeth's lines his own. Striking, though, is the fact that the exemplary life he sketches is not the self-sacrificing prisoner on Robben Island, but rather the comfortable bourgeois ideals of South Africans in the twenty-first century. Asked if he would choose the same passage again today, Daniels confirms his continued 'enchantment' with those lines and Shakespeare's concern, as he puts it, 'with the insignificance of man' and the truth that, 'in the final analysis, we are nothing' (Hahn interview, 3 February 2010). This is not exactly a 'political' reading of Shakespeare, in the sense that the word has been used in Departments of English roughly since Daniels countersigned Macbeth's speech, although its *Nachträglichkeit* speaks of a projective reading towards a future politics in which the ideals of the struggle against Apartheid are sullied by the all too worldly nature of the new society. (I will return to this in Chapter 3.)

'My co-mates and brothers in exile'

In neither Hahn's nor Desai's interviews is the question of a political reading of Shakespeare broached directly. Saths Cooper declares that he 'focused on more serious works rather than the comedies because this was a political prison' (Hahn interview, 5 February 2010). Yet a quarter of the prisoners chose passages from the comedies, belying their status as 'less serious' plays, while almost a fifth preferred the sonnets. Besides, the question of the 'seriousness' of a passage, poem or play becomes highly contestable in such a context.

Govan Mbeki's passage in the Robben Island Shakespeare – an apparently surprising choice for the man who had rivalled Nelson Mandela for the position of leader on Robben Island, and who stuck to an implacably radical communist position – is Orsino's opening disquisition on love, music and desire in *Twelfth Night*.[13] Perhaps Mbeki had internalized Orsino's lines from high school and in circumstances of acute and chronic sensory deprivation the poetic celebration of poetry and love spoke to a condition that was every bit as serious and political as the ferocious ambition of Macbeth or the deprivations of Lear. What might have counted was not the relevance of Shakespeare's thoughts but rather their *irrelevance* to the prison – their evocation, as poetry, of a 'world elsewhere' – although the evocation of yearning and desire and the painful sweetness of such craving is indubitably part of Orsino's speech.

Wilton Mkwayi saw in Malvolio's eager response to what he supposes to be Olivia's hortatory invitation to embrace greatness not the comic gulling of an ambitious fool, but rather a serious meditation on the nature of resolve and leadership – '[B]e not afraid of greatness. Some are born great, some achieve greatness, and some have greatness thrust upon them' (*Twelfth Night*, 2.5.132–4). In this context of thwarted longing, Hahn rewrites in his play the story told to him by the South African actor John Kani that Mkwayi had waited 23 years to marry his fiancée:

> (*Flipping through the 'Bible' and finding the passage from*) Wilton Mkwayi. (*Pause.*) He goes to prison just before he marries his wonderful fiancée. He waits for over twenty-three years on Robben Island. Finally to stand in front of the pastor to be married. He marries after he is released, so they are perpetually engaged for

> over twenty-three years. They did visit. Once a month, once every three months. (*Upstage, Wilton sees his wife arriving on the island.*) A visit is *so* irregular. They are not meant to make the prisoner comfortable. Sometimes the boat would arrive with the men's wives and the men are ready; and the boat turns back. (*Wilton begins to weep quietly as he is returned to his cell.*) Men come, take a look at their wife and march back to their cells without talking (figure 1.4).[14]

Two members of Mandela's 'isolation' section on Robben Island, Elia Motsoaledi and Kwedi Mkalipi, a member of the opposing PAC, chose Puck's enchanting apology at the end of *A Midsummer Night's Dream*:

> If we shadows have offended,
> Think but this, and all is mended,
> That you have but slumber'd here
> While these visions did appear.
> And this weak and idle theme,
> No more yielding but a dream. (Epilogue, 1–6)

Like many of his comrades, Motsoaledi received little more than a primary-school education before taking part in ANC protests. He joined *Umkhonto we Sizwe* (MK), the armed wing of the ANC founded and headed by Nelson Mandela. He was one of the Rivonia trialists with Mandela, Sisulu, Mbeki and others. He is unlikely to have studied the play at primary school. What appealed to him and Mkalipi about these lines? Had they done the play at school? Had they had the same whimsical fantasy that offense might be overlooked if it were discounted as a mere dream? The suggestion that one may enchant away an experience not to one's liking by thinking of it as little more than a dream? Or the promise of friendly solidarity and restoration with which the play slips into an awakening reality? Or was it simply the magic of Shakespeare's words, lightening

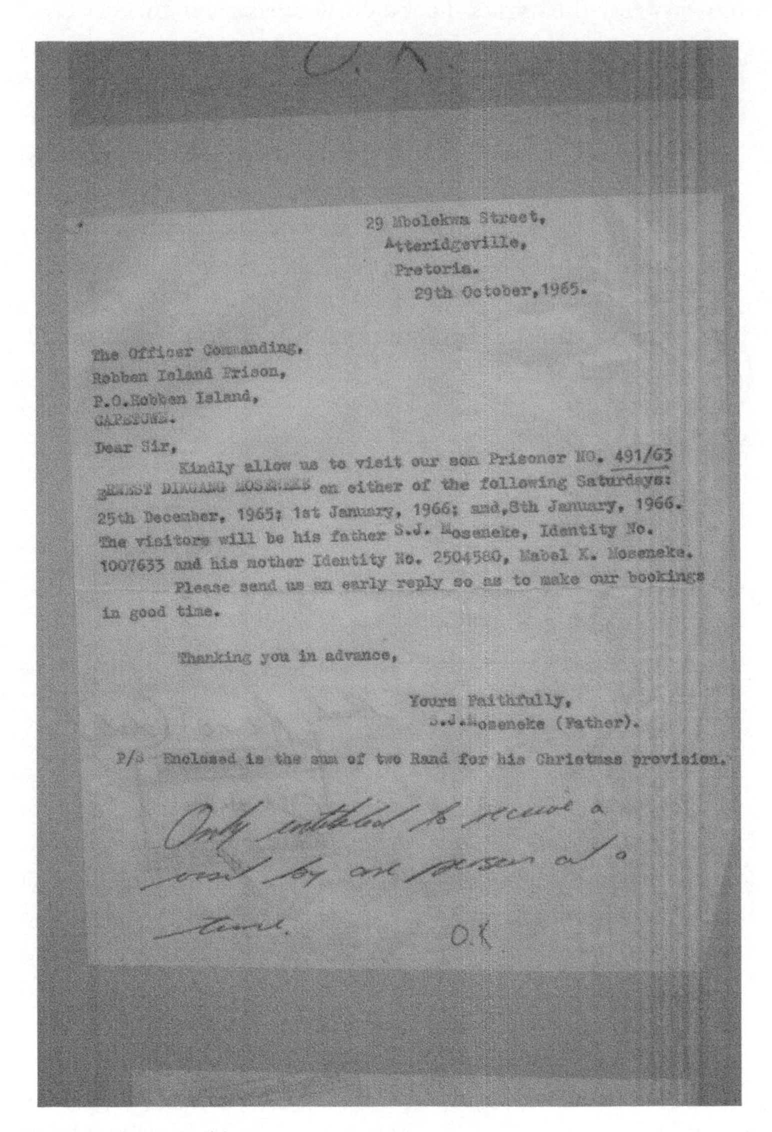

O.K.

29 Mbolekwa Street,
Atteridgeville,
Pretoria.
29th October, 1965.

The Officer Commanding,
Robben Island Prison,
P.O.Robben Island,
CAPETOWN.

Dear Sir,

Kindly allow us to visit our son Prisoner NO. 491/63 ERNEST DIKGANG MOSENEKE on either of the following Saturdays: 25th December, 1965; 1st January, 1966; and, 8th January, 1966. The visitors will be his father S.J. Moseneke, Identity No. 1007633 and his mother Identity No. 2504580, Mabel K. Moseneke.

Please send us an early reply so as to make our bookings in good time.

Thanking you in advance,

Yours Faithfully,
S.J.Moseneke (Father).

P/S Enclosed is the sum of two Rand for his Christmas provision.

Only entitled to receive a visit by one person at a time.

O.K

Figure 1.4 Typed letter.

for a moment the dreariness and emptiness of the prison? I have no way of knowing. Motsoaledi died in May 1994, on the day that his fellow prisoner, Nelson Mandela, was inaugurated as the first President of the democratic South Africa for which they had fought and suffered.

In an interview in 2008, Mkalipi rejected his earlier choice of Puck in favour of Lady Macbeth's lament, 'All the perfumes of Arabia will not sweeten this little hand' (*Macbeth*, 5.1.49), saying that *this* was the moment in Shakespeare that appealed to him:

> That, ah, whatever could have been done, nothing could ever purify this system of Apartheid and so then therefore, when, then she says, 'All the perfumes of Arabia will not sweeten this little hand', it meant then that you could bring everything in but the damage that is done by the system of Apartheid can never be repaid. And that is why it was said, the people was saying, 'Let us go and kill the people who have done this.' It makes one want to kill them in order to get out of this. Because nothing can ever bring justice to what has happened to us. So that is the system that it was.[15]

The move from an actor's plea to be excused to a revolutionary's reflection on the need for retribution means that for Mkalipi at any rate, time out of prison had increased a sense of indelible injustice, and that this need for revenge is underwritten by a fresh reading of Shakespeare.

That three members of the B-section cells selected passages from *As You Like It* makes it more than likely that they had shared the play as a prescribed school text, but their choices of individual passages speak of different personal and ideological affinities with Shakespeare's play.

Sandi Sijake, an MK cadre who became a Major-General in the new South African National Defence Force and is currently President of the ANC Veteran's League, showed an extraordinary degree of prescience in choosing Orlando's opening complaint[16]:

> As I remember, Adam, it was upon this fashion bequeathed me by will but poor a thousand crowns, and, as thou say'st, charged my brother, on his blessing, to breed me well; and there begins my sadness. My brother Jaques he keeps at school, and report speaks goldenly of his profit. For my part, he keeps me rustically at home, or, to speak more properly, stays me here at home unkept; for call you that keeping for a gentleman of my birth that differs not from the stalling of an ox? His horses are bred better; for besides that they are fair with their feeding, they are taught their manage, and to that end riders dearly hir'd; but I, his brother, gain nothing under him but growth; for the which his animals on his dunghills are as much bound to him as I. Besides this nothing that he so plentifully gives me, the something that nature gave me his countenance seems to take from me. He lets me feed with his hinds, bars me the place of a brother, and as much as in him lies, mines my gentility with my education. This is it, Adam, that grieves me; and the spirit of my father, which I think is within me, begins to mutiny against this servitude. I will no longer endure it, though yet I know no wise remedy how to avoid it. (*As You Like It*, 1.1.1–22)

At a time when the turn to theory and politics in Shakespeare studies was in its infancy, and indeed when Shakespeare's comedies were still considered a lesser genre, this soldier chose a play steeped in questions of the arbitrary exercise of power, disinheritance, relations between master and servant and access to land. The conditions of which Orlando complains bear obvious parallels with those suffered on Robben Island, while the 'spirit of my father' that the younger son invokes, which 'begins to mutiny against this servitude', would have resonated with the broader sprit of rebellion against the servitude imposed by Apartheid. At the same time, Orlando's speech concerns a falling out between brothers, and the determination by one brother, through fear and jealousy, to denigrate and subjugate another. This is as pertinent an aspect of Orlando's speech as its resistance to servitude and disinheritance, and perhaps reflects internecine conflicts in an institution where the political rhetoric at least was to accommodate everyone as brothers.[17]

The other choices from *As You Like It*, by Mobbs Gqirana and J. B. Vusani, respectively, are the Duke's celebration of the 'sweet' 'uses of adversity' in the exile of the forest, and Jacques's famous enumeration of the seven ages of man. Whereas Sijake recognizes something of his own condition in Orlando's resistance against imposed servitude, Gqirana highlights the more conventional celebration of the honesty and moral rigours of adversity:

> Now my co-mates and brothers in exile,
> Hath not old custom made this life more sweet
> Than that of painted pomp? Are not these woods
> More free from peril than the envious court?
> Here feel we not the penalty of Adam,
> The season's difference. As the icy fang
> And churlish chiding of the winter's wind,
> Which when it bites and blows upon my body,
> Even as I shrink with cold, I smile and say . . .
> Sweet are the uses of adversity;
> Which like the toad, ugly and venomous,
> Wears yet a precious jewel in his head;
> And this our life, exempt from public haunt,
> Finds tongues in trees, books in the running brooks, and good
>   in everything.
> I would not change it. (2.1.1–18)[18]

Duke Senior's sentiments form a common narrative in almost all accounts of the experience of Robben Island: not merely in the experience of exile from the 'common haunt', but also the bitter cold of the winter and even sometimes the summer months when the dreaded 'South-Easter' blew, and especially in the celebration of honest comradeship and the judgement that the prisoners had finally made the Island their own – wresting from its privations a sense of individual and common growth and achievement. Mandela quoted the lines 'Sweet are the uses of adversity' in a letter to his wife in June 1970, remarking: 'the chains of the body are often wings to the spirit. It has been so all along, & so it will always be'.[19]

This triumphalist narrative contrasts, however, with Vusani's choice of Jaques's speech, which echoes Daniels's perception of the universalized nihilism of Macbeth. Daniels's 'with nothing . . . with nothing . . . with nothing' reprises Jacques's 'Sans teeth, sans eyes, sans taste, sans everything' (2.7.166). Gqirana disappeared without a trace after his release from the Island. He is the putative victim of the death squads that an increasingly vicious and desperate security apparatus unleashed on the country in the 1980s.[20]

That Walter Sisulu should have gravitated towards Shylock's insistence on a shared humanity in *The Merchant of Venice* is not surprising:

> Hath not a Jew eyes? Hath not a Jew hands, organs, dimensions, senses, affections, passions, fed with the same food, hurt with the same weapons, subject to the same diseases, healed by the same means, warmed and cooled by the same winter and summer, as a Christian is? If you prick us, do we not bleed? If you tickle us, do we not laugh? If you poison us, do we not die? (3.1.52–9)

But it is difficult to know whether Sisulu gave full weight to the contrary aspect of Shylock's appeal, in which the lesson of a common humanity lies not in equality or companionship but rather a common propensity for retribution: 'and if you wrong us, shall we not revenge?' (3.1.60). Recall that such retribution is the subject of Mkalipi's declaration above that 'the damage that is done by the system of Apartheid can never be repaid . . . It makes one want to kill them in order to get out of this. Because nothing can ever bring justice to what has happened to us'.

The difficulties with the kind of reading I am offering are that there is no way of telling how each of these readers viewed the play as a whole – or even whether they read the whole play. Did Vusani, for instance, notice Shakespeare's ironic placing of Jacques's nihilist vision against the entry of Orlando, the master, seeking sustenance for his servant, Adam, or did he merely recognize an old platitude, uncontextualized by the rest of the play?

If we take their chosen passages together the result is a *communal* reading in Shakespeare's comedy, in which the love story is displaced or negated by its framing social circumstances: of the abuses of privilege and power, brotherly jealousy and conflict, the capacity to learn from and transcend adversity and a reflection upon the cycle of human life that emphasizes its ambitious vanity. *As You Like It* in this bare reading shows its latent affinities with *King Lear*.

'The weight of this sad time we must obey'

Three prisoners saw in Shakespeare's harrowing tragedy of royal hubris, the cruelties of power, and familial nastiness countered by loyal service something that spoke to and of their conditions on the Island. Two of them, Justice Mpanza and Mohamed Essop, chose exactly the same passage: Edgar's closing declaration of paradoxical obligation and freedom, in which the burden of tragic events turns out to be the expression of personal feeling rather than obedience to conventional expectation or demand: 'The weight of this sad time we must obey; / Speak what we feel, not what we ought to say. / The oldest hath borne most; we that are young / Shall never see so much, nor live so long' (5.3.323–6).

With only a primary school education, Justice Mpanza joined *Umkhonto we Sizwe* (MK). He went to the Soviet Union for military training, and was captured and sentenced to a 15-year sentence on Robben Island. Sampson offers this account of the arrival of Mpanza and his comrades on the Island:

> The morale of the ANC prisoners depended heavily on hearing good news from the outside, which at first was rare, but in 1967 more guerrillas arrived on the island with exciting stories to tell of having actually fought in Southern Rhodesia as members of the "Luthuli detachment," who were trying to get through to South Africa. One of thc commanders of MK, Justice Mpanza, joined the isolation section and Mandela as first Commander in Chief was filled with pride to hear the accounts of the bravery and training of the troops, even though the incursion had failed. (Sampson, 211)[21]

Mpanza would therefore have read *King Lear* with the experience of real armed conflict, torture and capture. And in an interview after his release he gives a disturbing account of his encounters with the 'boer' soldiers, as he calls them, whom his group has taken prisoner. On two occasions at least, his group executed their prisoners. This is his account of one of them:

> During the first battle there was one boer whose name was Thomas. He was a mercenary. He was amongst those we had captured . . . we kept Thomas in the spotlight because it was said he was a notorious mercenary from Port Elizabeth. *Hawu*, when he cried, asking us to spare his life we did not. We shot him dead. *Ya*, he cried and said, "Don't kill me, don't kill me", whilst he was injured . . . *Ayi*, we dealt with him.[22]

Part of the practical difficulty faced by guerrillas who have infiltrated a country, and whose chief aim is to remain undetected, is that they have no infrastructure for the care of enemy wounded or prisoners of war. So it made sense to kill them. Nevertheless, the interview betrays the ANC's transgression of one of the most fundamental provisions of what Shakespeare, in *Henry V*, calls 'the laws of war'. How might Mpanza have considered King Henry V's controversial order: 'Then every soldier kill his prisoners' (*King Henry V*, 4.6.37) during the battle of Agincourt?

'Once more into the breach, dear friends'

Henry V is the play from which Ahmed Kathrada chose his scene. It is Henry's exhortation to his troops at Harfleur, now a cliché of militarist bombast. Most people know only its first line, 'Once more into the breach, dear friends. . . .' Few can continue with its conditional 'or close the wall up with our English dead', and fewer still, I suspect, recall its tension between courage as a matter of willed performance dictated by the demands of the moment and the appeal to an achieved nobility through the equation of the legitimacy of blood with a willingness to go to war:

> In peace there's nothing so becomes a man
> As modest stillness and humility;
> But when the blast of war blows in our ears,
> Then imitate the action of the tiger:
> Stiffen the sinews, conjure up the blood,
> Disguise fair nature with hard-favoured rage
> [. . .]
> Dishonour not your mothers; now attest
> That those whom you call'd fathers did beget you.
> Be copy now to men of grosser blood,
> And teach them how to war. (3.1.3–9 and 21–4)

The open appeal to English nationalism of Henry's final rallying cry, 'Follow your spirit; and upon this charge / Cry "God for Harry! England and Saint George!"' (33–4), would presumably have had some resonance in the general sentiments of courageous pulling together for a common cause. The speech is uncharacteristic of Kathrada as a person, judging from his letters, memoirs, the testimony of others and his generally proclaimed delight in Shakespeare as a whole. Considering that he filled seven prison notebooks with quotations from Shakespeare, and had a fully annotated copy of the complete works, this choice indicates the *public* nature of Venkatrathnam's invitation. There was presumably a felt pressure to choose not merely lines that had an immediate personal appeal, but which would speak of Shakespeare's work as the site of common resistance and mutual struggle. It would therefore have made sense for Kathrada to choose this speech as an invocation of mutual, publicly declared solidarity while reserving other moments in Shakespeare for himself or for sharing with his family.

The 'TV generation'

Both mutuality and resistance were to become a site of a different kind of struggle at about the time that the Robben Island Shakespeare was making its rounds among the tightly knit members of B-section, many of whom had been on the Island for almost 15 years. Twelve years after Mandela and his Rivonia trialists arrived on Robben Island – after a long, difficult and protracted process, which resulted in the relaxation of the harshest, most brutal, and indeed lawless, regime in the prison (so that, as Buntman puts it, 'these men had come to have a pragmatic understanding of resistance' (Buntman, 113)) – the prison received an influx of new revolutionaries: young, brash, impatient and absolutely sure of their cause, who had started the momentous uprisings that began on 16 June 1976. Mandela comments that 'in terms of our ordinary lives . . . an ordinary warder . . . could be more important to us than the Commissioner of Prisons or even the Minister of Justice . . . the best way was to influence officials privately rather than publicly' (Mandela, quoted in Buntman, 114).

The large numbers of new, extremely radicalized young men, for the most part members of the Black Consciousness Movement, who arrived on the Island from 1977 onwards challenged such private accommodations and the pragmatic approach to prison conditions which they implied. Appalled by and contemptuous of their older leaders' 'meekness', they sought confrontation at every turn – with the existing prisoners as well as the warders. For Mandela as initiator of the armed struggle and Commander in Chief of MK, 'to be perceived as a moderate was a novel and not altogether pleasant feeling' (Mandela, *Long Walk*, 577).

In his autobiography Mandela is fairly sanguine about the conflicts of the late 1970s, stating that with patience they were finally accommodated to more conventional and more mature views: 'I wanted these young men to see that the ANC was a great tent that could accommodate many different views and affiliations' (Mandela, *Long Walk*, Kindle loc. 8766). Others were not as generous. Natoo Babenia dismisses them as the '"TV generation" because they were born when television came to South Africa. They had seen too much American trash, liked it and became Americanised. They were not of the caliber of the older generation.'[23] This is hardly a fair comment, considering the intense ideological commitment of the new prisoners (who could be said to be 'American' only in the sense that their opposition to racism was shared by the marginalized and oppressed of US society, who through the Civil Rights movement and the Black Panther movement had actively opposed racial prejudice), and the brazen courage with which they refused to bow to the order of the prison. But Babenia does give voice to a resentment shared by many of the older prisoners.

The other selection from *Henry V*, by Sibusiso Bengu, who became Minister of Education in Mandela's first cabinet, is unusual, but it may be explained by the new challenge to the settled order and authority of the older prisoners. It is almost always cut in performance, and I doubt whether even seasoned Shakespeareans recall it with any clarity. It is the summation of one of Shakespeare's most perplexing and long-winded pieces of political rhetoric and expediency, the Archbishop of Canterbury's sycophantic disquisition in God's name on Henry's right to go to war against France:

> Therefore doth heaven divide
> The state of man in divers functions,
> Setting endeavour in continual motion;
> To which is fixed as an aim or butt
> Obedience. For so work the honey-bees,
> Creatures that by a rule in nature teach
> The act of order to a peopled kingdom.
> They have a king, and officers of sorts,
> Where some like magistrates correct at home;
> Others like merchants venture trade abroad;
> Others like soldiers, armed in their stings,
> Make boot upon the summer's velvet buds,
> Which pillage they with merry march bring home
> To the tent royal of their emperor;
> Who, busied in his majesty, surveys
> The singing masons building roofs of gold.
> The civil citizens lading up the honey,
> The poor mechanic porters crowding in
> Their heavy burdens at his narrow gate,
> The sad-ey'd justice with his surly hum,
> Delivering o'er to executors pale
> The lazy yawning drone. I this infer,
> That many things, having full reference
> To one consent, may work contrariously.
> As many arrows loosed several ways
> Come to one mark, as many ways meet in one town,
> As many fresh streams meet in one salt sea,
> As many lines close in the dial's centre;
> So may a thousand actions, once afoot,
> End in one purpose, and be all well borne
> Without defeat. (1.1.183–213)

Bengu failed to indicate the date of his choice but, since there are no dated signatures before 1975 or after 1977, it is likely that he would have read Venkatrathnam's Shakespeare shortly after the new, extremely disruptive arrivals on the island.

At first sight a traditional encomium on authority and an ordained system might not seem to be the *immediately* striking aspect of the Shakespeare *oeuvre* to a revolutionary whose primary aim was to overthrow a regime which had itself acted and spoken in the name of order and obedience. But since most of the inmates of section B (who signed the Robben Island Shakespeare) were members of the older, 'meeker' generation, it is likely that Bengu would have chosen the Archbishop's speech – with its emphasis on order and a sense of common purpose driven by ordained obedience – because it reflected a political and metaphysical problem of maintaining unity and command on the island after the disruptive influx of the 'young lions'. In the light of this challenge to the achieved hegemony of the ANC leadership on the Island after the early conflicts with members of the PAC, the elderly Archbishop's sentiments might have spoken powerfully of the need for unity in diversity and firm control of the energies of the revolution.

'Words in pain'

Henry V offered the opportunity for the expression of general, public sentiments of warlike courage and ideological community; Shakespeare's much more introverted and troubled history of a weak king's fall from power in *Richard II* speaks to its readers of more personal truths. Mac Maharaj, one of the most celebrated of the Robben Island circle and a close confidant of Mandela (and who continues to be involved in the government of South Africa as spokesperson for President Jacob Zuma), marked the dying Gaunt's lines:

> Where words are scarce, they are seldom spent in vain;
> For they breathe truth that breathe their words in pain.

> He that no more must say is listen'd more
> Than they whom youth and ease have taught to glose. (*Richard II*, 2.1.7–10)

These four lines resonate in a number of ways with what a prisoner on Robben Island who had been there for some 12 years might have thought or felt. The date, July 1976, coincides exactly with the new, youthful uprisings, but Maharaj would probably have known little of them, and the rebels would not yet have arrived on the Island. What the lines do convey is an ascetic sense of inherent truthfulness, not only of verbal reticence but also the compelling nature of words spoken in pain. This may be regarded as a reflection of the intrinsically convincing character of speech through suffering – in Maharaj's case, the suffering imposed by the prison itself and the concomitant sacrifices of political struggle. His choice thus echoes Duke Senior's speech on the sweet uses of adversity, in which suffering the pangs of cold and exposure finds 'tongues in trees, books in the running brooks, / Sermons in stones, and good in every thing' (*As You Like It*, 1.2.16–17).

Gaunt, in illness and pain, arrogates to himself, in the form of a *general* aphorism, the *individual* voice of truth. But the aphorism lends itself to different voices. There are three competing aphorisms in Gaunt's lines: one, that the laconic is necessarily closer to the truth than the garrulous; two, that speech emitted in pain is necessarily true; and three, that age is more truthful than youth. All of these aspects of folk wisdom are projected proleptically onto a narrative that will cohere around the figure of Nelson Mandela about Robben Island as the crucible in which the new 'rainbow nation' would be formed: of the Island as the place of truth forged through pain and achieved through the discipline that comes with age and wisdom.

In this context, however, the unconscious overtone of truth achieved through torture is hard to ignore. Especially in the case of Mandela, but also of Robben Island memoirs as a whole, the suggestion of torture and its relation to truth and speech in the passage from *Richard II* tends to be suppressed. Mandela hardly mentions torture, and when he does it is in the abstract, as an instance of a catalogue of the injustice and brutality of Apartheid as a whole. When Kathrada offers examples of actual cases of torture in a recorded conversation, Mandela is strikingly laconic:

KATHRADA:	Then, of course, there's also hostility against other police who tortured . . . our people.
MANDELA:	Yes . . .
KATHRADA:	A chap like Mac [Maharaj], for instance. I don't know if he'll ever agree to [come], because Swanepoel . . .
MANDELA:	Tortured him?
KATHRADA:	Ja . . . Andimba [Toivo ja Toivo], very badly too.
MANDELA:	Mmm.
KATHRADA:	Zeph [Motopeng].
KATHRADA:	A lot of people were tortured by him.
MANDELA:	Mmm. (Mandela, *Conversations*, 399–400)

The context of this conversation is a proposal that a number of former security police officers should be invited to join their former victims at a social gathering – specifically a barbeque or 'braai', the culinary icon of Afrikaans culture. Here are Mandela's eager words: '*Who* can we get, man? Because, you know, it's such an act of generosity . . . to say to these fellows, can we have a braai?' (398).[24] Mandela's subsequent reticence as Kathrada begins his roll-call of the tortured may arise from the sudden reflection of what it might actually mean to bring torturers and their victims together at a meal that was synonymous with a masculinist Afrikaner culture. But it also speaks of a general silence around the trauma of torture, itself reflected in the anodyne unfolding of a barely acknowledged litany in dialogue, as if what happened could not be told by a single person or conveyed in any but the blandest terms: 'because Swanepoel . . . MANDELA: Tortured him? KATHRADA: Ja . . . very badly too. . . . KATHRADA: A lot of people were tortured by him.'

This dialogue about torture, or rather about avoiding the truth of torture, and which moreover comes as an addendum or supplement to both Kathrada and Mandela's considered, official autobiographies, is symptomatic of both a necessary forgetting of the past – a different kind of necessary suppression – and also the unspeakability, as Elaine Scarry reminds us, of torture itself. In Scarry's analysis, pain marks the limits of language and the obliteration of the world for the victim. Torture exemplifies the asymmetry of the relation to pain of the person who does and the person who doesn't have it: it is the marker of absolute certainty for the person who experiences it, while for anyone else it is the marker of doubt: *I* cannot have *your* pain, and because pain takes no object (unlike the hunger *for* food, or the sight *of* the sky, there is no thing that pain is *of* or *for*); it therefore has no sharable referent in the social world of language and the realm of shared objects.[25]

Mandela and Kathrada's anodyne conversation about the victims of Swanepoel's systematic torture signals both the unspeakability of torture as the inflicting and experience of pain and the general silence, in the Robben Island memoirs and literature as a whole, about pain as an object of experience. Scarry cites Virginia Woolf's observation that 'English, which can express the thoughts of Hamlet and the tragedy of Lear has no words for the shiver or the headache . . . The merest schoolgirl when she falls in love has Shakespeare or Keats to speak her mind for her, but let the sufferer try to describe a pain in the head to a doctor and language at once runs dry,'[26] in support of the fact 'that physical pain does not simply resist language but actively destroys it' (Scarry, *Body*, 4). The radical solipsism that this signals means that the experience of pain is the irreducible limit of the social, the shared, the communal.

The forgetting of torture and its unspeakability thus marks an essential failure of both the proclaimed communality and the spirit of resistance celebrated in the standard memoir. Nor is Shakespeare of much help. Shakespeare himself tends to avoid direct representations of torture and the experience of physical pain. A notable exception is the putting out of Gloucester's eyes in *King Lear*; but a similarly horrific scene, when Hubert prepares hot irons to blind the young prince Arthur on the orders of King John, is averted when, as the king's servant, he has a change of heart. Lavinia's entrance in *Titus Andronicus* is truly horrifying, but the rape and mutilation occur off-stage, and the response of audience and especially Marcus's elaborate poetic response drawn from Ovid in Act 2 Scene 4, exemplify our virtual incapacity to 'communicate the reality of physical pain to those who are not themselves in pain' (Scarry, *Body*, 9). It therefore signals pain as a marker of the essential otherness of all human beings to each other.[27] In other Shakespeare plays, torture and painful punishment are alluded to or promised, but not depicted or enacted: the villains in *Much Ado about Nothing* and *Othello* are threatened with 'brave punishments' in the closing lines, and even Caliban's pinches and stings in *The Tempest* are anticipated or recollected rather than actually suffered.

None of the scenes from Shakespeare that evoke or allude to pain and torture were marked by any of the prisoners on Robben Island. It is impossible to say why this is so, but it is plausible that, just as the prisoners were ready to tell and retell stories of communal suffering during hard labour in the quarries but reticent to speak of their individual experiences of torture, the few scenes of torture in Shakespeare, if they were read at all, would have been found to be unbearably appropriate.

The most recent of the Robben Island memoirs, Sedick Isaacs's *Surviving in the Apartheid Prison: Robben Island: Flash Backs of an Earlier Life* (published in 2010, some 20 years after the last prisoner left the island), is one of the few not only to deal with torture,[28] but also to acknowledge the incapacity to speak of the experience and record the debilitating feelings of embarrassment and humiliation that the experience retained for its victims long after it had ceased:

> I thus underwent the same experience that many others in the same situation in South Africa went through during that period,

> the same experience of trauma, batons, arm twists, the same sense of anxiety compounded by uncertainty and the same guilt for leaving one's family . . . Nobody I knew who went through these experiences freely talks about it. I certainly never could.[29]

Scarry insists on the phenomenology or metaphysics of subjective isolation in torture, but Isaacs assumes a shared condition of pain and humiliation: he represents himself as simply one of many subjected to the same systematic procedures of the South African Special Branch, and he assumes that each person subjected to such procedures would have suffered in the same way, endured the same degrees of pain, anxiety and shame. In brief, Scarry argues that the inaccessibility of another's pain is what drives human beings apart; Isaacs suggests that the universal human susceptibility to pain is what unites us.

Isaacs's story differs from the other Robben Island accounts insofar as it claims no coherent teleology of resistance or narrative of collective endurance: he offers no more than 'flash backs of an earlier life' that have left their marks on him in the form of recurrent anxieties, phobias and hallucinations. In fact, Isaacs's is a peculiarly individual set of experiences, since even as a prisoner kept in the communal cells (and therefore apart from Mandela and his comrades) he suffered a much greater degree of punishment on the island. Singled out as a 'trouble-maker', he spent a number of stretches in the solitary confinement cells called the 'culukoet' (or 'cooler', sometimes spelled 'kulukoet'), including an uninterrupted 11-month period of isolation: he was subjected to intense loneliness and painful discomfort in a cell too small for either standing upright or lying fully stretched out – it was unbearably cold in winter; he had barely enough food to stay alive; and was subjected to prolonged sensory deprivation. Isaacs registers as no one else the ways in which the body may be harnessed to torture itself – how it is possible to 'make the prisoner's body an *active* agent, an actual cause of his pain' (Scarry, *Body*, 47).[30]

Incarcerated in the general section, Isaacs was not able to sign Venkatrathnam's Robben Island Bible; he was probably unaware of its existence. Had he been able to do so, what might he have chosen? *King Lear* offers itself as a likely choice. Certainly Kent's time in the stocks, about which critics tend to pass over very quickly, but which must have been an excruciating instance of the capacity of the body to punish itself through imposed immobility and exposure, although Shakespeare hardly dwells on such pain by imbuing Kent with Stoic insouciance: 'Some time I shall sleep out, the rest I'll whistle' (2.2.151). I would like to think that Isaacs might also have sympathized with Edgar as Poor Tom, a member of the cosseted ruling class, dispossessed of everything except the bare forked animal of the body, and forced to test the limits of human need. 'O, reason not the need!', Lear cries in bewildered anger and despair to his daughter, 'our basest beggars are in poorest things superfluous' (2.4.264–5), and thereby sets the stage for his plumbing of the ultimate needs of the bare human body and spirit.

What might this mean in what we call 'real life'?

'Reason not the need'

In January 1982, after completing an MA in Shakespeare at the University of York in England, I returned to South Africa, first to get married, and then in short order to take up a teaching post at the Rand Afrikaans University (RAU) in Johannesburg, a university founded to provide an ideological space for Afrikaan students in opposition to the English-speaking, liberal University of the Witwatersrand. The English Department at RAU was small but active, intensely committed under its pioneering head, Stephen Gray, to fostering the cause of African and South African literatures in opposition to the then largely Leavisite departments at the English universities.

It was the custom at RAU to throw the scraps that few senior professors wished to teach to the newest members, and so upon my arrival I found myself preparing not *King Lear* but rather *Joseph Andrews* in my first year of teaching. My wife and I settled in a nearby suburb, renting from an anti-Apartheid activist lawyer a house close to the university in an up-and-coming, Chelseafied suburb being converted from its formerly white working-class origins to a new bourgeois chic. We had scarcely moved in with our meagre 20-something possessions – a double mattress for the floor, some cane chairs, a pine dining-room table and chairs, an inherited oriental carpet, some bookcases made of planks and bricks and prized posters of Picasso, Renoir and student productions of *Henry IV Part I* and *The Revenger's Tragedy* – when, one rainy dusk, there was a knock at the door. A young black man, barely more than a boy, stood on our threshold: he introduced himself as Doctor (he had been baptized 'Doctor'), and asked if we had any space in our back yard for him to sleep. He had probably been sizing the joint, as they say, for while we shook our heads vehemently, declaring that we had no such shelter, in truth we had.

Taking up a quarter of the space between our back kitchen door and the boundary of the property there was indeed a room of sorts: it had a roof of corrugated zinc, through which one could see the sky like the Milky Way, a door, a small window and a bare cement floor. It had no running water or toilet. It had been originally built to accommodate a domestic servant, who would have spent six days out of seven, twelve hours a day, cleaning, cooking and taking care of the children of the 'master' and 'madam' who occupied the house. When we took over the rent it was, as it were, derelict, and we could not imagine, nor did we want, a stranger living there. Where would he eat, where would he relieve himself and wash, and, in any case, who was he? In all conscience, we asked our landlord, who had impeccable anti-Apartheid credentials, and he confirmed that we had our right to our privacy, whatever the political circumstances of the country at large.

The following week I was conducting a seminar on *Joseph Andrews*, and I happened to have chosen for discussion the scene from chapter XII, in which Joseph, having been set upon by robbers, beaten and stripped naked, cowers at the side of the road, trying to persuade a coach to take him to the nearest town. Readers of Fielding's novel will recall that each passenger in the stagecoach finds a self-serving reason to refuse Joseph entry, until finally a technical legal argument persuades them to allow the naked, shivering wretch to ride on top with the postilion, who is the only person prepared to offer the victim his coat.

The discussion took its usual course, invoking Fielding's sharp social satire and an all-round condemnation of the immoral selfishness of the occupants of the coach. Many of my students lived in the nearby suburb of Triomf ('Triumph'), which had recently been built for exclusive white habitation on the cleared ruins of Sophiatown, from which all the original black inhabitants had been forcibly removed. But we all agreed in our round moral condemnation of Fielding's characters and our sympathy for poor Joseph. Half way through this discussion the image of the young man knocking on our door asking for shelter came unexpectedly, and shockingly, to mind. What difference was there, I thought, between me and the pompous lawyer or the hypocritical lady so concerned with her modesty that she would leave a naked, bleeding boy by the side of the road? At home that evening I told my wife of the class, and we shared a feeling of abject shame and moral misery. Would that Doctor come back, we thought. The gods were merciful. He did. He stayed with us for the next 7 years.

Our experience – a minor, fortuitous opportunity for white South Africans to extend a modicum of compassion to a dispossessed black youth – is dwarfed by the example of Sol T. Plaatje, one of the most remarkable men to have come out of South Africa. Born not far from where I grew up, but 75 years earlier, Plaatje was a pioneering African journalist, editor and politician. He was the first secretary-general of the African Native National Congress (precursor of the ANC), and the first black South African to write a novel in English. In the early part of his adult life Plaatje was a court interpreter who spoke nine languages; a spokesman and ambassador, both for the African people at large and his Barolong community, who travelled extensively in South Africa and to the United States, Canada and England. He was an historian who began writing his *Boer War Diary* at the age of 23;[31] a pamphleteer whose 15-page account of inter-racial sexual relationships in South Africa sold 18,000 copies when it was published in New York in 1921;[32] a linguist who co-produced the first Setswana phonetic reader;[33] a translator who wrote *Sechuana Proverbs and their European Equivalents*;[34] a political writer who produced a damning account of the effects of the Native Land Act of 1913 in *Native Life in South Africa*;[35] and a Shakespearean who translated five-and-a-half of the Bard's plays into Setswana and published 'A South African Homage' in Israel Gollancz's commemorative collection, *A Book of Homage to Shakespeare*,[36] which he helped edit.

In 1913, the Native Land Act, in a single stroke, dispossessed all Africans of their land. It made it illegal for them to own any land outside a demarcated system of reservations or 'homelands' that comprised 13 per cent of the territory and, in an attempt to force African sharecroppers into the cities to work on the gold mines, made it illegal for them to own any livestock on land now rendered 'white'. The Act, which went into effect in the middle of a bitterly cold winter in 1913, saw thousands of families forced overnight to leave their shelters and livelihoods and seek, along strange roads and unwelcoming farmsteads, some form of sustenance and shelter. Plaatje travelled the length of these rural areas, in a kind of Cobbett's 'Rural Rides', recording the iniquity and misery caused by the new law.[37] One of the most poignant moments he records is of his coming across a startled family at the side of a public road, hurriedly and secretly burying a young son who had died in the bitter cold along the way – forced to steal a bare plot of public land in the middle of the night, since they had nowhere else to lay him to rest.

Especially pertinent is Plaatje's use of Lear's voice on the heath – some 70 years before Martin Orkin's seminal essay on the affinities between *Lear* and the mass dispossession of black South Africans of their land – to express Plaatje's own despair and anger at the brutal power of a law that dispossesses people even of a place to bury their children[38]:

> Are not many of us toiling in the grain fields and the fruit farms, with their wives and their children, for the white man's benefit? Did not our people take care of the white women – all the white women, including Boer *fraus* – whose husbands, brothers and fathers were away at the front [during the Anglo-Boer war] – in many cases actively engaged in shattering our own liberty? But see their appreciation and gratitude! Oh for something to –
>
> Strike flat the thick rotundity of the world!
> Crack Nature's moulds, all germans spill at once!
> That make ungrateful man! (Plaatje, *Native Life,* 147)

There is a certain irony that, in appropriating the voice of Lear, Plaatje in fact occupies the position of dispossessed authority, who ultimately concedes that he has 'taken too little care' of what 'wretches feel' (3.4.32–4). But what Plaatje's turn to Shakespeare at this moment of outrage signals is *King Lear*'s extraordinary combination of an anatomy of a specific political (dis)order and the metaphysic of basic human need.

In one of Scarry's most insightful moves, she writes of the ways in which 'in normal contexts', the room is the quintessence of civilization:

> While the room is a magnification of the body, it is simultaneously a miniaturization of the world, of civilization. Although its walls, for example, mimic the body's attempt to secure for the individual a stable internal space – stabilizing the temperature so that the body spends less time in this act; stabilizing the nearness of others so that the body can suspend its rigid and watchful

> postures; acting in these and other ways like the body so that the body can act less like a wall – the walls are also, throughout all this, independent objects, objects which stand apart from and free of the body, objects which realize the human being's impulse to project himself out into a space beyond the boundaries of the body in acts of making, that once multiplied, collected, and shared are called civilization. (Scarry, 38).

The bare shelter in which Lear, his fool, Gloucester, Kent and poor Tom are finally collected exemplifies, in its material and spiritual dimensions alike, the 'room' as Scarry describes it here, both as the space in which the body can stabilize itself from external harm and project itself in acts of communal making. Plaatje's witness to the unutterable cruelties of the South African Land Act, exemplified by the Lear-like scene of the family burying their son in terror and pain in the middle of the dark, wintry African veldt, speaks of the destruction of civilization as Scarry defines it, of legal dispossession as an act of complete barbarity.

Isaacs's experience of Robben Island in the isolation cells adds a further dimension. Scarry states that the room is the space of civilization only in 'normal contexts'. When it is turned into a prison or a torture chamber, the room effects the 'undoing of civilization, [it] acts out the uncreating of the created contents of consciousness' and rather than merely being the space in which torture takes place, it is 'an agent of pain' (Scarry, 39–40). Lear's fantasy of prison as a place in which he will at last be able to 'sing like birds i' th' cage' with Cordelia, of whom he'll 'ask . . . forgiveness', and where together they will 'live, / And pray, and sing, and tell old tales, and laugh' (5.3.9–12) is a dream of Scarry's picture of the room as the very condition of human civilization, in a place which, even if only in fantasy, he begins indeed to 'reason the need' of humanity.

This returns us to the closing lines of *King Lear*, chosen by two of the prisoners. The lines register, at least implicitly, the divide between the old who have suffered and the young who have suffered as witnesses to such suffering: 'The oldest hath borne most; we that are young / Shall never see so much, nor live so long.' A community is established through that 'we': one that has *lived through* and will *live on*, in both senses of *surviving* and *carrying* or *bearing further*.[39] But what is said, or what is to be said, is elided or obscured by the detour of an impersonal imperative that overrides a social obligation in favour of isolated subjectivity: 'The weight of this sad time we must obey; / Speak what we feel, not what we ought to say.' These events, from which there has been no escape, impose upon us the duty to speak what we – each *one* of us separately – *feels*. From the community of 'we' Shakespeare derives the isolation of what each feels separately; from the injunction to speak truly emerges silence – or else, no more than the promise of speech, after the play, when everyone has made his or her solitary way home, bearing the burden of the shared space of the theatre.

I have spent a disproportionate amount of time on *King Lear* not only because three prisoners found it significant,[40] but also because it speaks to the experiences of others on the island who did not have access to Venkatrathnam's Shakespeare. Of all Shakespeare's works it combines a representation of particular political forms of dispossession and concomitant suffering within a concrete grasp of the metaphysics of human need that resonate especially well with the struggle against political oppression and the absolute reduction – like Lear and Poor Tom on the heath – of the body and mind to their barest forms of existence. In the play, as on Robben Island, the specificity of the political is intertwined with the irreducible needs of the human.

The *I* of the Prison

A much more personal investment in Shakespearean sentiments may be found in other choices. Joe Gqabi's spare three lines from

Richard II register a tension between hope and despair that must (despite protests to the contrary in the official narratives) have been especially prevalent among long-term prisoners:

> . . . even through the hollow eyes of death
> I spy life peering; but I dare not say
> How near the tidings of our comfort is. (2.1.271–3)

It is surprising that no one marked one of Shakespeare's most striking representations of the real and imaginative responses to imprisonment, King Richard's reflections at the end of the play on the capacity of the human imagination to overcome the physical confines of incarceration. The stylized nature of the soliloquy, with its somewhat baroque metaphor of the mind peopled by thoughts and emotions likened to contrasting classes of an irreducibly early modern polity, may not have spoken directly to Robben Island prisoners who read the play. It does, however, convey the debilitating effects of solitary confinement, where the imaginative transcendence of isolation is the only form of solace available:

> *I* have been studying how *I* may compare
> This prison where *I* live unto the world;
> And, for because the world is populous
> And here is not a creature but *myself*,
> *I* cannot do it. Yet *I'll* hammer it out. (*Richard II*, 5.4.1–5)

With his incomparable facility, Shakespeare conveys, in the re-iterated return of the first person pronoun 'I', the inexorable centrality of subjectivity in its very attempts to transcend itself and reach a 'world elsewhere'. This 'I' is subjected to ironic pressure in variously punning forms throughout Breyten Breytenbach's *The True Confessions of an Albino Terrorist*, in the form of the 'Mr. I', who is both addressor and addressee of the memoir. But it plays less of a role on Robben Island, where the need to establish a community in the 'peopled' world of the prison is the overriding personal and communal concern.

Isaacs is the only writer who spent a long time in solitary confinement in the Robben Island punishment cells – to a degree that surpassed temporary punishment and constituted extended torture. He remarks that, 'on Robben Island solitary confinement was like being in a tomb' (Isaacs, Kindle loc. 2122). His account of the body as the passive measure of time in isolation is comparable to Richard's meditation on the same phenomenon:

> I wasted time, and now doth time waste me;
> For now hath time made me his numb'ring clock:
> My thoughts are minutes; and with sighs they jar
> Their watches on unto mine eyes, the outward watch,
> Whereto my finger, like a dial's point,
> Is pointing still, in cleansing them from tears. (5.5.49–54)

Stoic Transcendence and Guilty Complicity

Not surprisingly, *Julius Caesar* proved to be a popular choice. The page on which Venkatrathnam's Shakespeare was open for display when I saw it in Stratford was signed 'NR Mandela' with the date '16 December 1977', as it was in the British Museum exhibition, 'Shakespeare: Staging the World', in 2012.[41] Mandela's signature lines are Caesar's lofty pronouncement of stoic defiance and endurance:

> Cowards die many times before their deaths:
> The valiant never taste of death but once.
> Of all the wonders that I yet have heard,
> It seems to me most strange that men should fear,
> Seeing that death, a necessary end,
> Will come when it will come.[42] (*Julius Caesar*, 2.2.32–7)

Mandela found in Shakespeare multiple instances of comfort and resolution in the face of death and adversity. I have already noted his attraction to the line, 'Sweet are the uses of adversity', from *As You Like It*. The prospect of death was clearly something that spoke to him during the Rivonia trial, when the death penalty was a possible, even a likely, outcome:

> I was prepared for the death penalty. To be truly prepared for something, one must actually expect it. One cannot be prepared for something while secretly believing that it will not happen. We were all prepared, not because we were brave but because we were realistic. I thought of the line from Shakespeare: "Be absolute for death; for either death or life shall be the sweeter". (*Long Walk*, 445)

The superficial affinity between Mandela's situation and the Duke's advice is contradicted, however, by the Shakespearean character's cynical manipulation of Claudio. For the Duke offers the terrified condemned man an outlet in a nihilistic vision of death as a refuge from the emptiness of life. Mandela was ready to die because of the fullness of life – because of his dedication to a just, fulfilled existence for all people, and his attraction to three moments in Shakespeare that celebrate an achieved indifference to the vicissitudes of fortune speak of his achievement as a latter-day Stoic. It is quite possible that he learned the outlines of Stoical philosophy and action in part at least from Shakespeare.[43]

Mandela signed the passage from *Julius Caesar* the day after Toivo ja Toivo put his name to Peter Alexander's transcription of Hand D, – thought to be that of Shakespeare, in the manuscript of *Sir Thomas More* – which comes at the very end of Alexander's edition. Mandela therefore probably had the passage in mind before the book reached him. The date on which Mandela signed his name has a peculiar significance in the history of the colonial struggle between invading white settlers and the black population, and it would certainly not have been lost on him. Long marked as a sacred national holiday in South Africa before 1994, 16 December was known as the Day of the Covenant. It marked the victory at the Battle of Blood River, when some 5,000 Boer settlers (known as the Voortrekkers or Trekkers) defeated between 10,000 and 15,000 Zulu warriors in 1838 who attacked their laager. On the day before the battle, the Trekkers had made a covenant with God that, should they emerge victorious against these impossible odds, they would keep the day of the battle as a holy day. They did, and throughout my childhood 16 December was commemorated with church services and festival gatherings in specially demarcated parks called the '*Geloftefeesterrein*' that even the smallest towns and villages established throughout South Africa, many of them commemorated with granite monuments and replicas of the wagons used by the Trekkers in their journeys into the interior.

For someone who was so well versed in the history of the Afrikaners, and who continually invoked their struggle against British colonialism on behalf of the African nationalist cause, Mandela must have been aware that he was putting his name to Caesar's declaration of courage in the face of death on this, the most sacred day in Afrikaner political history. He would have recognized the extraordinary courage of the men, women and children who steeled themselves behind their *laager* of wagons to face Dingaan's enormous army of Zulu *impis*. But he would also have seen himself and his comrades in the mirror of such stoical determination.

Like so many who find aphorisms that speak to the specific conditions of their lives, Mandela pays little attention to the context of the speeches from which he draws his lessons or comforts. He appears not to heed the irony that he, the leader of a democratically oriented insurrection, who furthermore insisted on serving for only a single term as president of South Africa after Apartheid, should have chosen as his signature statement the arrogant self-assurance of the would-be tyrant, or that the words of wisdom and comfort that come to mind during his trial are those of *Measure for Measure's* ruler – a manipulative, Machiavellian politician.

Andrew Masondo's choice from *Julius Caesar* registers a much more personal affinity with a character trapped in the toils of political compromise. He chose Mark Antony's grieving, self-flagellating elegy delivered over Caesar's newly butchered corpse:

> O pardon me, thou bleeding piece of earth,
> That I am meek and gentle with these butchers!
> Thou art the ruins of the noblest man
> That ever lived in the tide of times.
> Woe to the hand that shed this costly blood!
> Over thy wounds now do I prophesy –
> Which like dumb mouths do ope their ruby lips
> To beg the voice and utterance of my tongue –
> A curse shall light upon the limbs of men;
> Domestic fury and fierce civil strife
> Shall cumber all the parts of Italy;
> Blood and destruction shall be so in use,
> And dreadful objects so familiar,
> That mothers shall but smile when they behold
> Their infants quartered with the hands of war,
> All pity choked with custom of fell deeds;
> And Caesar's spirit, ranging for revenge,
> With Ate by his side come hot from hell,
> Shall in these confines with a monarch's voice
> Cry 'Havoc!' and let slip the dogs of war,
> That this foul deed shall smell above the earth
> With carrion men, groaning for burial. (*Julius Caesar*, 3.1.255–76)

It is a curious speech for a revolutionary whose aim was to overthrow a tyrannical regime, but perhaps it was appropriate enough for a soldier who had joined MK in the early sixties, and returned to Moscow after his release from Robben Island for further military training. Masondo was, notoriously, later in charge of the ANC's own internment camps in Angola, the most renowned and reviled of which was called 'Quatro'.

The same generation that had suddenly upset the balance of Robben Island after 1976 was to cause considerably greater unease for the ANC in exile. Thousands of revolutionary youths left South Africa to join the ANC's military wing, *Umkhonto we Sizwe* (MK). Kept in military camps in Angola while the ANC attempted to use its unexpected new cadres strategically, those soldiers became restless. Many complained repeatedly of high-handed, even abusive, treatment by the ANC leadership. Discipline collapsed in the camps, where living conditions were extremely poor, and one of the camps underwent a mutiny. So ANC Security established its own internment camp, Quatro.[44] What one member of the older generation (Babenia) described dismissively as the Americanized 'TV generation', and another (Mandela) welcomed as a younger cohort to be converted, caused serious disciplinary problems in the MK ranks outside South Africa.[45] Quatro is not particularly well known. It is less famous or notorious than its island cousin. Although the ANC established a number of commissions of enquiry in the nineties, few senior members other than Nelson Mandela were happy to have the appalling conditions and treatment of its prisoners made public.[46] Thabo Mbeki attempted to suppress the findings of the Truth and Reconciliation Commission (TRC) with regard to Quatro. The same brutal conditions that marked the early years of Robben Island as a political prison appear to have been duplicated and even intensified at Quatro: arbitrary beatings by guards, torture, the lack of proper food and in some cases no bedding whatsoever for months on end, and backbreaking labour, sometimes leading to death.

The name of the camp was derived from a notorious Apartheid prison, and the isolation cells were called after their counterparts on the much better-known Island some 2,000 miles to the South.

There was one difference, however. The Apartheid regime paid some attention to the rule of law. Suspects were indeed detained without recourse to law and tortured in police stations, but once found guilty by a court of law they could in theory appeal to the technical impartiality of the law and prison regulations. Mandela especially made a point of using the law against the institution in this way. Many of the improvements in the living conditions on Robben Island came as a result of such strategic appeals, pursued with especial rigour by Mandela in his capacity as a trained lawyer. As Moodley writes, 'we knew the prison regulations backwards, and we used every clause in the prison regulations to be able to defeat the warders'.[47] But there appear to have been no prison regulations of this sort at Quatro. Many detainees were held without charge, and few could look forward to a definite release date. Treatment was arbitrary, like that of the lepers on the Island before it became a political prison.

The events at Quatro may be explained by adducing the peculiar conditions of the ANC in its war with the Apartheid government – its vulnerability to infiltration by spies and *agents provocateurs* and the lack of understanding by the 1976 generation cadres of the ANC's political strategy and the need for military and political discipline – but it remains as the dark alter ego of Robben Island. It is both obscured by the light that has recently been cast on the more famous prison and remains as a blot on the recent triumphalist symbol the Island has become.[48]

Viewing Mark Antony's guilt-ridden soliloquy over Caesar's body in the light of this context, it is tempting to see in Masondo's recognition of a friend's guilty betrayal, wrapped in the invocation of bloody revenge that denies the most natural of instincts to pity – 'That mothers shall but smile when they behold / Their infants quartered with the hands of war, / All pity choked with custom of fell deeds . . . Cry "Havoc!" and let slip the dogs of war' – a proleptic concern not only with division but with an internecine conflict that employs the most brutal means to put down internal rebellion.

Masondo would probably not have known Plutarch's account of Mark Antony's treatment of Cicero (omitted by Shakespeare), whereby Caesar's friend not only ordered Cicero's death, but also had his hands and head nailed above the *rostra* of the senate – where, as Plutarch notes, they presented a 'dreadful spectacle to the Roman people, who thought they did not so much see the face of Cicero as a picture of Antony's soul'.[49]

'A tide in the affairs of men'

Liloo Chiba ('Michael Dingake observes that Chiba was the most generous person he had ever met' (Kathrada, *No Bread*, 320)) was struck by Brutus's conviction of the necessary timeliness of political action:

> There is a tide in the affairs of men
> Which, taken at the flood, leads on to fortune;
> Omitted, all the voyage of their life
> Is bound in shallows and in miseries.
> On such a full sea are we now afloat,
> And we must take the current when it serves
> Or lose our ventures. (4.3.216–22)

Again, one is not sure whether Chiba chose this passage (in December 1977, like Mandela and Kathrada) for its resounding sense of a moment needing to be grasped, or for its more nuanced reflection of the incipient falling out of revolutionary comrades. The apparently incontrovertible aphoristic or folk wisdom of Brutus's pronouncement is undercut by Cassius's dissent – by the fact that this is not an isolated instance of timeless wisdom, but a heated disagreement regarding the strategy and tactic of the moment. The key word in the exchange is 'will', a reference to Brutus's stubborn insistence that his take on the situation is the correct one. It is not so much that the friends disagree, but rather that the previously weaker Brutus now sweeps aside Cassius's reasons to the point at which the instigator of the revolution gives way with hardly a fight. To Brutus's abrupt 'There is no more to say', Cassius responds with a craven 'No more. Good night' (227). Furthermore, Brutus's inclusive use of 'we' in 'We'll along ourselves and meet them at Philippi' (251) is a sham: it signals his careless obliteration of Cassius's considered judgement before his own. The outcome proves to be disastrous to the cause.

That was not true of the final outcome of Mandela's negotiations with the Apartheid regime, but Chiba's selection does look forward to the intensely disputed tactics that marked the prisoners' relationships on Robben Island, and even more significantly when Mandela decided to talk to the South African government after he had been isolated from his comrades in Polsmoor Prison. He declared that while he knew that they would oppose his decision, 'I knew that my colleagues upstairs would condemn my proposal. There are times when a leader must move ahead of his flock . . .' (Mandela, *Long Walk*, 523–4).

Very few of Shakespeare's Roman plays are on the list of works that caught the interest of the Robben Island comrades. The three instances from *Julius Caesar* are joined by only one more from the Roman oeuvre: Thompson Daweti's signature at the end of *Antony and Cleopatra*. It is unclear whether it marks the whole play, or just Caesar's final encomium to Cleopatra and Antony: 'She shall be buried with her Antony; / No grave upon the earth shall clip in it a pair so famous. High events as these / Strike those that make them; and their story is / No less in pity than his glory which / Brought them to be lamented' (5.2.355–60). *Coriolanus* goes unremarked, as does *Titus Andronicus*. Their potential role was occupied by the now famous production on Robben Island of Jean Anouilh's version of *Antigone*, in which Mandela played the part of Creon.

He subsequently reflected on the play's lessons for leadership and resistance:

> Antigone rebels, on the grounds that there is a higher law than that of the state. Creon will not listen to Antigone, nor does he listen to anyone but his own inner demons. His inflexibility and blindness ill become a leader, for a leader must temper justice with mercy. It was Antigone who symbolized our struggle; she was, in her own way, a freedom fighter, for she defied the law on the grounds that it was unjust. (*Long Walk*, Kindle loc. 8200)

To whom does Polynices's body belong? It is a question of which law prevails: the law of the state or the law of the gods? The prisoners on Robben Island were claiming the priority of the law of the gods over that of the state.

'This island's mine'

To whom did Robben Island belong? This question returns us to the claim that, as Buntman puts it, '[a]t the heart of prisoner resistance was the development of mechanisms to remove . . . state control of the prisoners and introduce prisoner self-government instead, on both a community and organizational basis' (Buntman, 265). In symbolic terms, Robben Island has clearly become the icon not only of resistance to Apartheid but also of the emergence of a new polity from its ashes. Buntman again:

> By material and geographic fiat, Robben Island is at the margins of the antiapartheid struggle and South Africa itself – the regime presumably chose the prison for its geographic marginality, and marginal it could have remained. However, in large part because the prisoners interpreted or resignified their time in prison as

> central to the historical trajectory of the national liberation struggle, they strove to make the Island a university of politics; thus, they were able to transform its place in history and its meaning in space and even geography . . . The prisoners, with the help of their allies outside the prison, were able to win the ideological struggle over what Robben Island came to mean in both anti-Apartheid politics and South Africa's nascent democracy. (Buntman, 264 and 268)

The question is whether the appropriation of symbolic and material power by the prisoners in the form of resistance could transcend the shaping conditions of the prison, thereby producing a wholly new order, or whether, as Daniel Roux has powerfully argued, the prison necessarily impressed itself as a shaping force upon the emergent order.[50] Isaacs's hallucinations and phobias 30 years after his release are merely one, psychological form of testimony to that necessity. In structural terms, if the prisoners enforced their own ideological state apparatus (to use Althusser's terms) to maintain ideological control within the institution, then the Quatro camps in Angola were a more ominous mirror image of the Island's controlling hand.

On 14 December 1977, two days before the book was signed by Mandela, Billy Nair marked a passage from the first play in the First Folio, an order that Alexander followed for Venkatrathnam's edition, *The Tempest*: 'This island's mine, by Sycorax my mother, / Which thou tak'st from me' (1.2.331–2).[51] It is as direct and uncompromising a claim as one might find in Shakespeare: Caliban the dispossessed, incarcerated upon an outcrop of rock and sand and heather that is rightfully his, subjected to tortures, forced into slave labour, announces his dispossession unflinchingly by using the derogatory 'thou' of his putative master: 'mine . . . my mother . . . thou . . . me'. The opposition of 'I' and 'thou' is empowered by the mediation of the claim to possession, the island through the mother: *my* mother, *my* island (Figure 1.5).

Figure 1.5 Exterior fence showing Freedom sign.

At a time when almost all South African students, at university and school (and indeed students in the English-speaking world as a whole), would have been taught Shakespeare's last singly authorized play as a representation of the conflict between the 'vile' and the 'non-vile', the 'noble' and the 'savage',[52] a prisoner on Robben Island registered Caliban's claim simply, as his own, and that of all the dispossessed inhabitants of South Africa. In doing so he anticipated a generation of Shakespeare criticism and scholarship.[53]

Chapter 2
Hamlet's Dreams

On 19 August 1981, Nelson Mandela made the following entry into his diary:

> Anthony Bobby Tsotsobe, 25
>
> Johannes Shanabgu, 28,
>
> David Moise
>
> Sentenced to death by Judge Theron (Charl). 'Long live the spirit of the toiling masses, long live the spirit of international mankind, long live NM; long live Solomon Mhlangu.'[1]

About 10 years later I was teaching a course on South African prison writing at the University of Cape Town. The course attracted South African students interested in the relationship between politics and literature, American study-abroad students and a new group of black students, sometimes ANC members, who as former MK cadres had been given scholarships to go to university. We were reading a poem by Jeremy Cronin, a member of the South African Communist Party, who had himself been imprisoned for some 10 years for political activities (though not on Robben Island). The poem, entitled 'Death Row', celebrated the MK prisoners, sentenced to death, who were kept in Pretoria Central Prison before their execution:

> Of course we never get to speak, as such, to each other.
> We're still fifty yards, one corridor,
> Many locked locks, apart.

Nkosi sikelel', we try singing, at night,
Us down here, to you, three condemneds, along there.
. . .
Then it's you singing slow
Antiphonal phrases,
Three tongues floating over
    That audible
Drop that gathers,
The words thrumming in your
Throats, brothers,
    About which
Some Wednesday morning
    Three nooses will go.
. . .
    Three voices
Called or
    Moise
Combine or responding
    Tsotsobe
Weaving
    Shabangu . . .[2]

Condemned political prisoners were not kept on Robben Island, but rather at Pretoria Central Prison, which housed the gallows. They were therefore a thousand miles away from their comrades on the Island. White political prisoners were usually incarcerated in a smaller, neighbouring prison, Pretoria Local, where they were a stone's throw from the condemned cells. For a while they were moved to Central, where they would have had some distant contact with the condemned prisoners, who traditionally spent their time singing until their execution.[3] In his poem, Cronin celebrates the potential for solidarity made possible by the reverberant spaces of the prison and the community of song.

In the discussion with my students, the question arose regarding the accuracy of Cronin's account. Were white prisoners not kept in an entirely different prison? Would the singing of the death-row prisoners have been accessible to those in the white cells, and vice versa? Did this really happen? In the midst of an earnest discussion, which had divided the class, a quiet, reserved man put up his hand. *I think Cronin is right,* he said. *This did happen.* A pause. *I was there; I am David Moise.*

Silence. We all stared at David. I glanced at my class list and wondered, stupidly, why I had not noticed. I cannot recall what we said after that. I remember only being overwhelmed by feelings of confusion, inadequacy and amazement that a man who had been on death row had chosen to attend my class on the very core of his experience.

On reflection, I have always been struck by the fact that this revelation was provoked, not by the many memoirs of imprisonment on Robben Island, but by a poem. It is a poem that puts the traditional opposition between the lyrical and the communal voice into play. All of Cronin's poetry does this. He deliberately uses verse to put *I* under pressure, showing how it is essentially communal, even in its most intense moments of isolation. 'Three now as one', Cronin writes, '*Th-a-a / Inta / nasha –na-le / yoonites tha / hooman / reiss*', mimicking voices that are not, naturally, his own, and weaving the individuality of their accents into the community of socialist aspiration and common humanity. That mimicry is rehearsed in Mandela's diary entry: *Long live the spirit of the toiling masses, long live the spirit of international mankind, long live NM; long live Solomon Mhlangu.* Mhlangu and many others did not survive. Moise – I am a happy, bewildered, grateful witness to this fact – did.

So did Evelina de Bruyn, whose story unfolds on the cusp of the transition from the old South Africa to the new. I turn to De Bruin because as a woman her story and experience are radically different from those of the male prisoners who were condemned to death. In this chapter I want to explore, via Shakespeare's tragedy, *Hamlet,* the gendered nature not merely of the South African prison system, but also of the subject and subjected *I* of imprisonment. De Bruin offers a point of departure in her contrast with men like Moise.

In 1989, shortly before the release of Mandela and his comrades from Robben Island, a group of 14 inhabitants of the small, arid town of Upington were found guilty of murder, under the doctrine of 'common purpose', for being present in the crowd when a municipal policeman was driven out of his house and killed. The *New York Times* at the time commented that 'They are the largest group of people sentenced to death here for a politically motivated crime within memory.'[4] The story speaks to differences in treatment, condition and experience, especially between men and women, and also of the mark made by the shadow of the gallows.

Like David Moishe, Evelina de Bruin spent months on death row. Unlike him and his comrades, she did so alone. Illiterate, thousands of miles from her family, removed from her children who by law were prevented from visiting her, and with her husband on death row, too, but removed from her in the male section, her life dwindled into a slow, despairing emptiness: 'dying just a bit, every day'.[5] In an interview with a priest, Evelina conveyed her sense of utter isolation, bordering on despair, starkly contrasted to the sense of community celebrated on Robben Island and even among the male prisoners on death row in Pretoria: 'You know, on death row, you hear the prison. *You* see the prison. *You* see the people going to prison. *You* see the people coming out of prison again. But in the death cells it is a different story. . . . there is no one there to have regrets and sympathy for you. You are just *finger alleen*[6] and you talk to yourself and you talk to God' (234; emphasis added). What is notable is de Bruin's contrast between the *you* of her interviewer, able to enjoy freely changing perspectives on the prison especially through sight, and the constrained world of the single, isolated woman on death row, for whom participation in a world beyond the death cell is impossible. Forced to confront a picture of herself imposed upon her by a system in the toils of which she is utterly powerless, there is no *we* for de Bruin, just an isolated and isolating *I*.

The Lyrical *I* versus the Dramatic *We*

The last group of signatures in the Robben Island Shakespeare was made against sonnets – the texts in which Shakespeare comes as close as he ever does to speaking in the first person. Six out of 32, almost a fifth of the total, encompassed this speaking *I* as if it were their own. There are reasons for surprise, but also for accepting such choices as natural. Surprise comes from the nature of lyric, especially the lyric steeped in the Petrarchan tradition that would have been utterly foreign to both the education and experiences of most Robben Island prisoners.

For some, confronted with a book of some 1,500 pages that they may not have encountered before, units of only 14 lines might have seemed more manageable than whole plays, whose language and literary codes may also have been foreign. A third advantage of the lyric is that it accommodates the voice of the person reading it – its address is transferrable to the moment of reading or recitation, so that an individual poem may, at a particularly striking, if evanescent, moment, speak for the person reading it. That is precisely what Cronin's poetry achieves: it musters the natural, personal voice of the lyric in the cause of community.

The exceptional Robben Island prisoners (like Dennis Brutus) who chose to express their experiences of the prison in lyric form, employ a mode of expression through which subjective experience of imprisonment can release conceptions of the self in its relation to the environment that more ideologically or communally controlled prose narratives are forced to suppress. The most pressing of Brutus's poems speak powerfully *against* the clinical resolve to preserve the disinfected commitment to pristine revolutionary identity – whether in the form of what is repressed or passed over in Mandela's spotless memoir or excoriated in Moses Dlamini's overt aversion to defined 'otherness' within the prison[7] – from contamination. Here is Brutus's honest acceptance of the way in which incarceration evokes the spectres of an *alter ego* that, like Hamlet, he might most wish to deny:

> In the greyness of isolated time
> which shafts down the echoing mind,
> wraiths appear, and whispers of horrors
> that people the labyrinth of self.
> Coprophilism; necrophilism; felatio;
> penis-amputation;
> and in this gibbering society
> hooting for recognition as one's other selves
> suicide, self-damnation, walks
> if not a companionable ghost
> then a familiar familiar,
> a doppelganger
> not to be shaken off.[8]

It is easy to overlook the unusual – indeed, brutal – honesty of this poem which, by adopting the lyric form rather than the more socially oriented narrative of the memoir, is able to admit and confront aspects of the self that tend to be occluded and suppressed through the communal reach of prose. Prisoners like Dlamini tend to vilify the common-law prisoners and the violent practices attributed to them – especially sexual – or gloss over them, as Mandela does. In characterizing the common-law prisoners as an even more perverted extension of the otherness of the white regime, Dlamini, for example, betrays a deep anxiety about possible contamination. Upon their removal, he remarks: 'Robben Island was rid for once and for all of these wretches – dregs of humanity who had been crushed by the system and had been brought by our political opponents to come and demoralise us, turn us into homosexuals and make us opt for Bantustans' (165). Mandela states that he saw the 'hardened criminals' from whom he insistently distances himself, 'not as rivals, but as material to be converted' (*Long Walk*, 484). Brutus, on the other hand, admits the perversions projected exclusively onto the criminal other as a haunting *alter ego*, an aspect of subjectivity that continues to betray the writing self, while the poet James Matthews, who was also imprisoned, acknowledges both a self invaded by spectres[9] and a possible affinity with the common-law prisoners from whom he is separated:

> I glimpse a field of shaven heads
> . . .
> in my isolation, I hear their sound,
> an orchestrated sound of maniacal laughter
> curses and cries of pain
> . . . . patterned bedlam
> it is the order of their day
> men with time to spare
> is their fate mine to share? (Matthews, *Poems*, 48)

This openness to alternative, darker aspects of subjectivity is arguably the function of genre as much as anything else, for all prison poetry registers a more prominently suffering, uncertain, haunted (the image is omnipresent) *I* as opposed to a more regulated *we*.

'Denmark's a prison'

Such haunting takes us to *Hamlet*, a play chosen by three of the Islanders. In this chapter I move from commentary on the Islanders' choices of particular passages to a broader discussion of the relationship between individual subjectivity and communal experience that is central to both the structural nature of the prison as such and the political project of the Robben Island prisoners in particular. Interrogating the critical focus on Hamlet as the archetype of modern subjectivity, I also subject the centrality of male subjectivity on Robben Island to questioning.

Interrogated by his friends, Rosencrantz and Guildenstern, who are in fact spying on him on behalf of the king, about what it is that ails him, Hamlet cries out: 'O God, I could be bounded in a nutshell and count myself a king of infinite space, were it not that I have bad dreams' (2.2.254–5).[10] In essence, this echoes Richard II's failed attempt to count himself a king through the imagination despite the reduction of his world to the solitary 'crushing penury' of his prison. This outcry extends Hamlet's sense, from the very beginning, that 'Denmark's a prison'. And it asks how what Hamlet calls his 'dreams' might help or prevent the extension of the prison into the world.

The most obvious affinity between *Hamlet* and incarceration is the prince's sense that Denmark itself is a prison. The prince feels not merely the confines of an enclosing space; he also anticipates Foucault's account of the Panopticon as the framing machinery of the modern state. The idea that a country might entomb its people materially or spiritually was a common refrain in Apartheid South Africa. It was a commonplace, grounded in material and not merely metaphorical reality, that prison was the lived condition of the majority of South Africans. Black South Africans found themselves in effect under house arrest in the country of their birth, as the appalling pass laws, which extended the Native Land Act of 1913, confined their legal domicile to a mere 13 per cent of the country: the 'Bantustans', or as the Apartheid regime would have it, independent, black 'homelands'. This meant that all black people, assumed to be the citizens of these ghetto territories at the stroke of a pen, were tolerated in 'white' South Africa as temporary guest workers. Since their work was essential to the economy of the country, and the comfort and privilege of whites, they were reduced to the status of itinerant, migrant labour, forced to carry 'passes' that could be demanded by any petty official, and which confined them to this slum or that. Failure to produce a proper pass frequently led to imprisonment. An astonishing proportion of the black population finally found themselves imprisoned as a result of these laws. South Africa was literally turned into a prison.[11] Their sense of incarceration thus occurred at three levels: the sweeping confinement of all black South Africans to impoverished rural slums far from any employment, health service, transport or proper schooling; the abiding apprehension of continuous surveillance and punishment for those who lived within 'white' South Africa; and the results of this system, which confined the near equivalent of the country's population to at least brief periods behind bars over the course of 40 years. For most black South Africans, then, South Africa was indeed a prison.[12]

How, then, do we in all fairness speak of the prison of Denmark and that of South Africa in one breath? Why should we want to do so? The prison on Robben Island penned its victims in with walls and bars, wire and gates, and ultimately, the sea itself. When Hamlet cries out, 'O God, I could be bounded in a nutshell and count myself a king of infinite space, were it not that I have bad dreams' (255–6), the conditional exemplifies his declaration that 'There is nothing either good or bad but thinking makes it so' (249–50): there is a kind of imprisonment that is essentially of the mind rather than the body. The injunction to remember, echoed in sonnet 122 – 'Thy gift, thy tables, are within my brain / Full character'd with lasting memory, / Which shall above that idle rank remain / Beyond all date, even to eternity' – and the ghost of Hamlet's father – 'Remember me' – seeks to avoid this psychological incarceration, with its acknowledgement that to be forgotten is to be enclosed, as in a tomb. The overriding aim of the Robben Island prisoners, repeatedly echoed in memoirs, autobiographies and interviews, was to resist imprisonment of mind and spirit through the confinement of the body.

What are Hamlet's dreams? He doesn't tell us, though we may guess. Whatever they are, they prevent him from escaping the confinement that he experiences as the condition of being in

Denmark – and of, course, because he is the son of the old king, of being Denmark itself. Being in and of Denmark prevents Hamlet from transcending or escaping his felt imprisonment through the imagination. His nightmares and obsessions imprison him within a peculiarly intractable kind of isolation or solipsism, but they are also a condition of *social* being in the troubled Danish court. Hamlet's peculiar experience of imprisonment within and by his dreams and the history of physical imprisonment in South Africa allow us to explore the possibilities of agency and the necessities of constraint at the interface of the personal and the political. This may be expressed grammatically as the dialectic of *I* and *we*, which always progresses via the exclusion of *they*. The problem that Hamlet formulates is that of human community and isolation within a polity – it is the issue at the heart of imprisonment for political causes.

The problem of solipsism – possibly the most harrowing aspect of being human – is encapsulated by Hamlet's sense of solitary confinement within his own dreams.[13] How is it related to the isolation of such South Africans as were placed in the 'kulukoets' or isolation cells of Robben Island, like Isaacs, or kept apart from the warmth of human society for years on end, like Breyten Breytenbach? And is the company of others not possibly a burden of its own – a kind of suffocating confinement? What, in other words, are the politics and the ethics of the need for community and what possibilities for action or agency do they allow?

'Mr. I/Eye'

Let's begin with Breyten Breytenbach's remarkable memoir, *The True Confessions of an Albino Terrorist*. The persona who speaks through the signature of the author opens by saying 'The name you will see under this document is Breyten Breytenbach. That is my name.' He addresses the memoir as a confession to a listener called 'Mr. Investigator', or simply 'Mr. I' (otherwise also 'Mr. Eye'):

> I'm sitting here – I have this little instrument in my hand; I have the earphones on my head and I speak to you and I listen to the voice coming back. And I learn from these words the reality as it is being presented at the moment of emitting the sounds. That is perhaps as close as I can come to what the identity is considered to be. That is as close as I can come to the truth. Here I am. Here the truth is also.
>
> I hope, Mr. Investigator, that that is what you expect of me. Because, you know, you could force me to deny whatever I say immediately after having said it: and you could probably force me to start all over again. I can tell you in advance that if I were to do that it would come out differently; it would be different; I'd no longer be there; I'd be somebody else as sincere, as keen to help, as obsessed by the necessity to confess.[14]

Breytenbach was, at the time of his arrest, trial and imprisonment for treason, considered to be the greatest living Afrikaner poet. He had left the country, and founded a political resistance group called Okhela, affiliated with the ANC, that sought to give white people an avenue actively to oppose the Apartheid regime. He returned to the country, in disguise, but was very quickly arrested by the security police. (Some speculate that he was betrayed by the ANC, which did not trust his maverick, white organization.) He was kept apart from all other political prisoners, including the other white activists. His interrogation took the form of being asked to write, repeatedly, the story of his life, in an attempt to demolish his assumed identity through the inevitable inconsistencies that constantly repeated narration would inevitably reveal. Breytenbach's interrogation was thus a parody of his profession as writer. As he presents his memoir, written (or dictated) after his release, it parodies his interrogation and confession: he records his 'confession' into a microphone to a Mr. Investigator who, in this case, is himself: 'Mr. I'.

I/You

Although Breytenbach was not tortured, he subjects the very idea of a stable identity that underlies the 'truth' to critique. Acknowledging the power of his interrogators to 'force him to start all over again', he insists that the inconsistency of repetition would simply affirm the radical instability of personal identity: 'it would be different; I'd no longer be there'. Because of his peculiar status as an icon of Afrikaans culture who had turned terrorist, Breytenbach was kept in isolation for at least 2 years before being transferred to Polsmoor Prison in Cape Town. The combination of his peculiar status as an '*albino* terrorist', his treatment by the Apartheid regime during his interrogation and trial and his long period of solitary confinement, means that his representation of imprisonment is more private, more insecure with regard to the filiations and affiliations of community and more focused on the instability and intractability of selfhood than other prison writing. In a set of representations in which there is hardly any manifestations of the community of first-person plural, the *I* is written under erasure: 'There is no "I", there is no name, there is no identity. But there are unchanging manifestations, habits, a hulk, a carcass, recognizable' (25).

By contrast, Robben Island prisoners sought to write *we* across every manifestation of personal identity, despite the prohibition of the pronoun by the prison authorities: 'The use of the word "we" was taboo in the censors' dictionary of usages. "We" meant that one had assumed, unlawfully, the role of spokesman for other prisoners' (Dingake, 167).

The circulation of Venkatrathnam's copy of Shakespeare presumably enabled the prisoners on Robben Island to recover themselves imaginatively in its fictional worlds. That is precisely why that book might have been considered dangerous by the authorities: why it and all other forms of literature were, at least in the initial years, strictly banned from the prisoners' lives. Only the peculiar, puritan respect of the jailers for religious difference offered a gap through which Shakespeare's works could pass as an allowed, sacred text that in the Apartheid vision of the world divided rather than united: Hindu from Christian, Muslim from Jew. Even when having books for the purposes of studying was permitted, the *sharing* of such texts was for a long time strictly prohibited. We may assume that the Complete Shakespeare that made its painstaking way from one prisoner to another on Robben Island provided, among other things, a sense of community within a system whose purpose was to isolate its subjects under a relentless, authoritarian gaze, and which permitted only the most minimal forms of human society. Shakespeare offered a world that could be shared in the imagination, to be sure – a world, we might say, of dreams; but the physical circulation of this book also bound each of its brief readers to their fellows through the accumulated, material traces of their names and singular marks upon its pages.

'Strip!'

In his reflections on his prison experiences in Pretoria Prisons in the 1960s, Hugh Lewin conveys both the despairing feeling of vulnerable isolation and its possible repair through the community of others especially well. Here is his description of his first, isolated entry into Pretoria Central Prison. Note especially the almost exclusive distancing of the experience in the ambiguous pronoun 'you', through which Lewin attempts to forge solidarity with his unknown reader against the alienated third person of the prison authority:

> Walking into a prison is like walking into a butcher's fridge, empty. It is cold – no curtains, no carpets, no heaters, nothing

> decorative, nothing unnecessary, just this long, dull corridor . . . Essentials only. You are stripped of everything inessential. You are stripped bare and given back only what they think is necessary. You are stripped bare of everything that you can call your own, constantly stripped bare of anything you can make your own; you are stripped bare in an endless process of peeling off your protective covering and leaving you naked. So they can watch you. So that you, like the corridor, are without decoration, without covering, with nothing behind which to hide, with nothing they can't see into and watch.
>
> 'Strip,' said the man with the three stripes on his arm.[15]

This word 'strip' encapsulates the process of being a prisoner.[16] It conveys precisely the Benthamite machinery of the Panopticon. No South African prison ever managed to exert in practice what Michel Foucault observes as a momentous shift in the Enlightenment from the ancient punishment of the body to the modern subjugation of the soul through a strict regime of incarceration; but that was not for want of trying.[17] Foucault claims that the new focus on the prison as the site of punishment, rather than the scaffold or the stock, constitutes a peculiarly horrible *invention* of the modern concept of the soul.[18] For all the privations of the body that are recounted in the South African prison memoir, this stripping of the soul is felt as the most acute kind of deprivation. Such deprivation takes material forms; it always works through the body – in the enforced nakedness experienced by Lewin; in the brutal body searches in Leeukop, the Fort and Robben Island prisons; in the coldness, harshness and bleakness of prison architecture, conveyed so powerfully by Brutus; in the monotonous badness of the food; and, perhaps most important, in the proscription of all forms of sensory, intellectual and emotional enrichment, including the banning of newspapers, books, conversation and music or singing. But its target is always the soul.

The classic text of South African prison experience, Herman Charles Bosman's *Cold Stone Jug*, conveys the craving for song as the essential expression of the soul's longings most movingly:

> There is something about these prison songs that haunts me. They seem to have been composed only for singing softly, five or six men standing in a corner, and one man standing a little distance off to say "Edge that" when a warder comes too near.[19]

D. M. Zwelonke declares of music that it 'was our much-needed food. We fed our spirits, fed them to the point where material food did not matter so much' (Zwelonke, *Robben Island*, 35). Albie Sachs writes about hearing a melody whistled by an unknown fellow prisoner in solitary detention: 'the urge for love and communication is the strongest of all drives. The thin line of music that connects me to the unknown whistler is more valuable to me than my food'.[20] Dingake comes to recognize the importance of music when he hears some distant piano music in the isolation cell: 'In the past I had been aware that I loved music . . . What I had never known was its soothing power, its power to assuage physical pain and mental stress. If music be the food of life, sing on' (Dingake, *Fight*, 156).

Song restores the protective layering that in Lewin's account is stripped away by the prison system; it relieves the relentless torture of sensory deprivation; and it forges a communality universally celebrated in prison memoirs. These prisoners' counter-intuitive experiences of what is or is not essential for human existence questions the distinction between the reality and the mere metaphor of imprisonment, especially in the context of the modern prison as the place in which the soul is shaped and controlled. With that in mind, let us return to *Hamlet*.

'I have that within . . .'

Literary critics have long argued that Shakespeare's tragedy marks the moment in the history of literary representation where the modern sense of human identity and selfhood as something essentially private or interior was first fully achieved.[21] Hamlet as a character gives us the first literary insight into the human self as a product of the mind or the heart, but also, crucially, as it expresses itself in language. This sense of inwardness as the site of selfhood is most vividly stated in the second scene of the play, where Hamlet, morosely and ostentatiously setting himself apart from the rest of the court in both manner and dress, is asked by his mother why he seems so unhappy. He pounces at once on that apparently innocent word, 'seems':

> *Hamlet* Seems, madam ! Nay, it is ; I know not seems.
> 'Tis not alone my inky cloak, good-mother,
> Nor customary suits of solemn black,
> Nor windy suspiration of forc'd breath,
> No, nor the fruitful river in the eye,
> Nor the dejected haviour of the visage,
> Together with all forms, moods, shows of grief,
> That can denote me truly. These, indeed, seem;
> For they are actions that a man might play;
> But I have that within which passes show –
> These but the trappings and the suits of woe.
> (*Hamlet*, 1.2.76–86)

Setting Hamlet's speech next to Lewin's description of his first encounter with the prison, and Breytenbach's less secure meditations on the status of the first person, we see a common anxiety to secure a sense of the self that transcends the uncertainties and pressures of outward form – of 'actions that a man might play' or mere 'moods, shows of grief'. But whereas Lewin fears the stripping away of what he calls 'nonessentials' until only a painfully naked interior remains, and Breytenbach accommodates himself to the idea that while 'there is no identity' there may be 'unchanging manifestations, habits, a hulk, a carcass, recognizable', such naked interiority, radically separated from all 'manifestations', is precisely where Hamlet tries to secure his true self: something *within*, as he puts it, which passes *show*.

Where does the true self indeed lie: hidden inside oneself, or embodied in deed? 'Indeed' or 'in deed' – really, genuinely, or in what one does? Let us turn to the moment when the world of the theatre is placed under the spotlight: when, delighted by the arrival of the players at Elsinor, Hamlet invites an impromptu performance from the chief player, who moves himself to tears with his passionate rendition of the scene of Hecuba's grief at her husband Priam's death. The young prince is both impressed and horrified by the intensity of the actor's show, which he finds 'monstrous'. It forces him to consider more deeply the relationship between personal integrity – that which supposedly 'passes show' – and the 'actions that a man might play' embodied in the theatrical passion displayed by the actor:

Now I am alone.
O, what a rogue and peasant slave am I!
Is it not monstrous that this player here,
But in a fiction, in a dream of passion,
Could force his soul so to his whole conceit
That from her working all his visage wann'd;
Tears in his eyes, distraction in's aspect,
A broken voice, and his whole function suiting
With forms to his conceit? And all for nothing!
For Hecuba!
What's Hecuba to him, or he to Hecuba,
That he should weep for her? What would he do
Had he the motive and the cue for passion
That I have ? He would drown the stage with tears,
And cleave the general ear with horrid speech;

> Make mad the guilty, and appal the free,
> Confound the ignorant, and amaze indeed
> The very faculty of eyes and ears.
> Yet I,
> A dull and muddy-mettl'd rascal, peak,
> Like John-a-dreams, unpregnant of my cause,
> And can say nothing : no, not for a king
> Upon whose property and most dear life
> A damn'd defeat was made. Am I a coward?
> Who calls me villain, breaks my pate across,
> Plucks off my beard and blows it in my face,
> Tweaks me by th' nose, gives me the lie i' th' throat
> As deep as to the lungs ? Who does me this?
> Ha !
> 'Swounds, I should take it; for it cannot be
> But I am pigeon-liver'd and lack gall
> To make oppression bitter, or ere this
> I should 'a fatted all the region kites
> With this slave's offal. Bloody, bawdy villain!
> Remorseless, treacherous, lecherous, kindless villain!
> O, vengeance!
> Why, what an ass am I! This is most brave,
> That I, the son of the dear murder'd,
> Prompted to my revenge by heaven and hell,
> Must, like a whore, unpack my heart with words,
> And fall a-cursing like a very drab,
> A scullion ! Fie upon 't! foh! (2.2.542–84)

When Hamlet tries to formulate or express the difference between his own condition and that of the mere actor – that is to say, when he asks what the actor would do if he had the *real interior* motive and passion that Hamlet feels within himself – *indeed* rather than merely *in deed* – he finds that his own response does not produce anything deeply profound, but rather the ranting and raving of a *bad* actor: a ham who can do no more than unpack his heart with words, as he puts it, like a 'whore'.

Hamlet stands here exposed to himself, stripped of the very interiority that he wants to preserve as his true being. If we step back for a moment from our involvement with the character Hamlet, and look at the technique with which that character has been created and presented, we will be struck by the fact that Hamlet's claim to be constituted by 'that within' which passes mere 'show', is being conveyed to us *by an actor*. Whatever feelings or thoughts the actor may harbour within himself as a real person are irrelevant to the composition of Shakespeare's character or to the expression of Hamlet's passion. It's *Hamlet's* passion that the actor expresses, not his own. And Hamlet's passion is a dream, a fiction: it is *all show*. Hamlet himself is no more than a collection of the actions that a man might play. The whole world of Shakespeare's profession – the theatre – shows that there are *no* actions that a man cannot 'play': put on, pretend, discard, in a dream, a fiction. These 'seem', literally, 'in deed'.

Does this mean that there is no interiority, no private world? Is the interiority that Hamlet claims itself no more than a dream?

In Hamlet's reflection on the working of the player's action he in fact suggests that interiority and performance are not totally separate: in 'forc[ing] his soul so to his whole conceit', the player is able to ensure that his 'whole function suit[s] / With forms to his conceit'. So, if Shakespeare creates, possibly for the first time, a sense of a real inner being in the figure of Hamlet he also shows that such interiority is no refuge, no real essence. It may itself be a kind of prison. It forestalls action; it robs Hamlet of the kind of agency – the capacity to transcend the constraints acting upon you from outside – which another of his nightmares, his father's ghost, demands of him. Hamlet is trapped within the confines of the prison that is Denmark because his bad dreams allow him no escape. At the same time, he discovers that the most social and public of the resources of human self-expression, language, has broken down, or breaks down as he tries to put it to use. The words that should enable him to forge and maintain the saving connections with others, and thereby sustain a secure sense of himself, seem to have emptied themselves of force and meaning. But this is true only of language as an expression of Hamlet's inner self. At the moments of most intense personal strain for Hamlet, the language of the play paradoxically flashes with a brilliance and intensity unmatched anywhere else in English. How can this be?

We need to distinguish here between language as a system, an impersonal machine as it were, that produces or releases meaning beyond the complete control of any single individual, and the capacity of individual speakers to find a way of expressing themselves through its system. It is when Hamlet tries to express *himself* through the system that he finds his way blocked. The way into that system for Hamlet, as it is for each of us, is through the personal pronoun *I*. The word *I* is the gap or the door that allows each one of us entry into the vast system of meaning that is the invention of none of us, singly or collectively, invented or created. Once we enter that impersonal system, through the gate of the pronoun *I,* we find ourselves both constrained and immensely empowered. First, we discover that *I* – the name we think of as uniquely our own, which refers to our inner being – is in fact not a name at all. Certainly it is not mine. But nor is it yours. Rather, it is a *shifter*: like other pronouns, it shifts its designation or reference in accordance with the ways in which each person appropriates the term for himself or herself at a particular moment of speech. Although I can now say *I* as if I were at the centre of the system, I find the moment I do so that there is no *I* without a *you,* no *we* without a *they.* In other words, before sociology, at the prior level of grammar, the self that appropriates the word *I* from language is constituted by its difference from others: *I* comes into being in contrast with *you, us* with *them.*[22]

But we also find that from the place that *I* affords us in the machine of language we can muster vast resources, in actions that transform the world and our relation to it, as we make promises, declare our devotion, bind ourselves in marriage and, if we are powerful enough, issue commands that end in life or death. 'Such', Shakespeare writes elsewhere, 'is the breath of kings' (*Richard II*, I.3.210–14). That each of us can appropriate the centrality of *I* to ourselves is dependent upon availability of that move to everyone else who speaks the language.

The Burden of *We*

Returning to Pretoria Prison after his sentence, Lewin exemplifies the discovery of the first person through its assimilation by and contrast to, others.

> We were now, officially, bandiete – full prisoners, out of detention . . . having been sentenced – and become bandiete, we returned to the same prison in the same way that we had done throughout our trial. We returned, in fact, straight to Du Preez's little office.
>
> 'Strip', he said.
>
> We took off our clothes and packed them, together with our watches, pens, pencils, writing-pads, books and remnants of the food-parcels – packed all the little things that made us private individuals, packed them into a suitcase for sending out . . . Du Preez handed us our new prison . . . uniform, brown and khaki . . . The clothes felt strange, heavy and unfriendly.
>
> We looked at each other and laughed. (*Bandiet,* 57)

In the emergence of the new pronoun, 'we', an experience that was previously harrowing is changed into an occasion for communal humour. The clothes remain 'strange, unfriendly and heavy', but the previously unbearable, corrosive gaze of the prison has been deflected and altered: 'we looked at *each other* and laughed'. Lewin's account recalls Hamlet's gnomic pronouncement that 'There is nothing either good or bad but thinking makes it so': that one could be 'bounded in a nutshell' and still count oneself the 'king of infinite space'. But Lewin also shows that such transformative thinking is not merely the product of the isolated individual imagination: it is discovered through the recovery of a sense of society that the prison seeks to destroy.

What appears to be a mere analogy between Hamlet's experience of his society as a prison and the actual incarceration of people within concrete and steel is made more than a likeness by the fact that the modern prison is designed to punish the soul or the mind as much as it does the body. Such punishment works by stripping the individual subject of all that appears at first to be 'inessential', but which finally turns out to be fundamental. There are times when music is more important than food, especially when its 'thin line' enables the ordinary support of human community and the resources through which it is sustained. Those resources are imaginative: they lie in a kind of thinking and feeling, which is why both Hamlet and the prisoner can take some solace in the thought that one could be 'bounded in a nutshell' and still count oneself the 'king of infinite space'. Exposed to the relentless eyes of court spies and a series of untrustworthy public displays, Hamlet thus feels as 'stripped' as Lewin or any other prisoner. But the communal identity that is repeatedly celebrated by South African political prisoners lies beyond the reach of the prince of Denmark. Exposed to a corrosive set of social relations, he turns inward: he claims an incorrigible inner self beyond public life that prisoners subjected to the ultimate mental torture of solitary confinement know is an illusion. One source of Hamlet's nightmares is thus his incapacity to find himself through the affirming touch of others. Hamlet's nightmares are, like those of Dennis Brutus on Robben Island and Breyten Breytenbach in Pretoria Prison, those of isolation.

We should, however, be careful not to accept the comfort of society too sentimentally or uncritically. It is commonplace for Apartheid political prisoners, especially those of Robben Island, to celebrate a complacent solidarity that hides its own forms of oppression and repression. When I asked the late Tony Holliday, who spent 7 years as a political prisoner in Pretoria Local Prison, to comment on the place of community in prison, he replied that prison did indeed render the need for other people unavoidable. But, he added, there is also no place that reveals so starkly the *burden* of that need. Holliday enables us to recognize and sympathize with Hamlet as he wishes to enclose himself within a private self that lies beyond the reach of public show. Communal life may be a different form of tyranny, itself a prison from which there seems to be no escape.

In her prison memoir, *Convictions: A Woman Political Prisoner Remembers*, Jean Middleton stands out for openly acknowledging the yoke of enforced society: 'it was inevitable that we should turn our misery and rage on each other. There is no doubt that we supported and saved each other, and that without each other we would have been lost, but our relationships very nearly destroyed us too.'[23] Barbara Hogan, detained and imprisoned for political activity, confirms Middleton's ambivalent sense of the undoubted need for and burden of society: 'it was both at once wonderful to have contact with people but enormously stressful. I think what I learned in that situation is that if you are going to have compassion for people then you have to have the ability to be human. You also need the circumstances to be human' (Schreiner, *Snake*, 25). As white women, Middleton and Hogan were in a much smaller group than the prisoners on Robben Island. Hogan recognizes that humanity requires a set of enabling circumstances, made extremely difficult if not impossible by the worlds of the Apartheid prison and the prison-house that is Denmark.

It is no accident that women should write with such candour about the difference between community and a group. Hogan remarks with regard to her own detention that 'it's not like on Robben Island where you're relating to a whole range of people, you know, you can like this one, dislike that one, like this one, that one's your chommie, this one you play guitar with. When there are just three or four of you, [you] are stuck with that. It's not a community, it's a group'

(Schreiner, 23–4). Middleton is scathing about the post-Apartheid tendency to valorize the experiences of male political prisoners at the expense of women. She remarks of an SABC interview with three male ex-prisoners aired in the mid-nineties: 'they were interesting interviews; but they weren't representative. It seems that the producer had chosen these three men to speak for all prisoners; and no-one seemed to have been chosen to speak for women' (118).

The silence and the silencing of women in the very name of social solidarity thus marks the world both inside and outside jail as a kind of continued incarceration, in the sense in which Denmark seems to be a prison to Hamlet, but not to his friends Rosencrantz and Guildenstern. We may see something of that entrapment by gender by looking at one of the incessant objects of fear and horror within the male prison: rape and feminization. Especially in the early years of Robben Island, when it was both a common-law and a political prison, political prisoners expressed a particular horror of the brutalizing effects of sodomy: of being forced to become, as it is put in prison cant, a *wyfie*.[24] Look at Moses Dlamini's response to the outcome of a fight between two prison gangs, in which the final stakes are sexual enslavement:

> The battle was over. [The losers] were now going to be the wyfies of the Big Fives . . . and tonight all three were going to . . . have taste of the domination that would make them submissive and dependent and never again dare fight against the Boer warders and the Big Fives. From now on they would be infused with feminine ideas and play the role of women in prison society. (*Robben Island: Hell Hole*, 58)

I am not disputing the accuracy of this prediction, but rather pointing to the uncritical assumption by the politically enlightened writer that submissiveness and dependence, brutality enforced by sexual violation, is the proper and natural role of women – the essential nature of what it is to be 'feminine' in the society *beyond* the prison.

There is a familiar tension in Dlamini's description: a characteristic that is thought to be intrinsic or natural turns out to be a set of performances that can be learnt or enforced.

Let us imagine, then, that in creating the character of Hamlet, Shakespeare represents the emergence of human consciousness as it finds its place in language through the slot of the *I*. But this representation of the self occurs under very peculiar circumstances, in which the social conditions that both enable language to bind people to each other and provide the space in which individuals are able to express themselves have broken down. Language is not merely an impersonal system that lies beyond us. We maintain it, shape it and change it minutely each time we claim our place in it; it is sustained and modified by countless forms of social practice. In the corrupt world of Denmark, language maintains an outward ordinariness, but, like the operation of language in the prison, distortions in the social practices from which language draws its life have begun to warp its words and their syntax. Oaths have lost their force; promises have been emptied of meaning; declarations are hollow; fictions have replaced reality; the sustaining bonds of marriage and allegiance have been dissolved in a welter of uncertainties and deceit; the security of personal relationships has been blighted by pervasive espionage; and tokens of love and devotion are redeployed to the ends of mean political intrigue. The very concept of the human is brought into question, as Strini Moodley notes in his choice, in the Robben Island Shakespeare, of Hamlet's balancing of the Renaissance humanist idealist against the more pessimistic, medieval perspectives on the nature of 'man':

> What a piece of work is a man! how noble in reason!
> how infinite in faculty! in form and moving, how
> express and admirable! in action, how like an angel!
> in apprehension, how like a god! the beauty of the
> world! the paragon of animals! And yet, to me,
> what is this quintessence of dust? Man delights not me. (2.2.305–7)

Alienated from the country he thinks of as his home, Hamlet finds himself estranged from his own language: he finds it, as Freud might have said, *Heimlich*: the dark side of the home: uncanny, strange, familiarly unfamiliar, nightmarish, like his dreams.[25] We may convey this alienation of language from the ordinary forms of human life in the Danish court by saying that Hamlet's Denmark is a society in which it has become impossible to say 'I love you'. Recall Hamlet's attempt, at the end of the play, to say these words. Enraged by Laertes's expression of grief and love, Hamlet steps forward, securely proclaiming his public identity as 'Hamlet the Dane', but then much less successfully tries to assert his personal identity as Ophelia's lover. Again, the pronouns tell us everything:

> What is he whose grief
> Bears such an emphasis, whose phrase of sorrow
> Conjures the wand'ring stars and makes them stand
> Like wonder-wounded hearers? This is I,
> Hamlet, the Dane.
> (*Leaps into the grave*)
> [. . .]
> I lov'd Ophelia: forty thousand brothers
> Could not, with all their quantity of love,
> Make up my sum. What wilt thou do for her?
> . . .
> 'Swounds, show me what th'owt do.
> Woo't weep, woo't fight, woo't fast, woo't tear thyself,
> Woo't drink up eisel, eat a crocodile?
> I'll do 't. Dost thou come here to whine,
> To outface me with leaping in her grave?
> Be buried quick with her, and so will I;
> And, if thou prate of mountains, let them throw
> Millions of acres on us, till our ground,
> Singeing his pate against the burning zone,
> Make Ossa like a wart! Nay, an thou'lt mouth,
> I'll rant as well as thou. (5.1.248–77)

The undignified brawl and ranting match literally over Ophelia's dead body show the degree to which the men who now strive to prove their love for the dead young woman are themselves trapped by the structures they have in part created and been shaped by. Desperate to prove a love that he feels *within* to the outside world, Hamlet is reduced to the most hackneyed clichés of romantic love. 'I loved Ophelia!' he proclaims, forgetting everything he has done and said that contradicts that claim.

Why should it matter so much to Hamlet at this point to declare his love – too late, in the past tense? Not only because he feels a sense of literally unutterable loss, but possibly because Shakespeare wants us to recognize his protagonist's own moral complicity in that loss. And despite Hamlet's alienation from the social world of Denmark, that world is the only place in which he can justify himself. Shakespeare shows us that, as his contemporary, John Donne, put it, 'no man is an island, entire to himself'.[26] But he also shows us that recognizing one's connections to the mainland of other people may be an intolerable burden.

It is especially so for Ophelia; it proves to be so for Hamlet. It is so for both of them because they find themselves members of a society in which the ordinariness of personal life has become impossible. *Hamlet* prompts to ask what ordinary life is, what it might be and why it should be preserved as something precious. So does the modern prison. One of the capacities of the ordinary is the saying to someone something simultaneously banal and momentous, intensely personal and also irrecoverably the property of others, traced and retraced with the *I* of strangers: 'I love you.' It requires one to be able to occupy a space made available by the countless uses of others, while making it uniquely one's own. Hamlet cannot do that. But nor can Ophelia. That is one of her unspoken nightmares.

Feminist scholars have observed that, on the margins of Hamlet's struggle with the patriarchal demands of the ghost, his fearful suspicions of his uncle's duplicity and his unbearable disgust at what he regards as his mother's gross sexuality, Ophelia is a curiously empty creature.[27] She, too, is hemmed in by social and familial relations that are as oppressive as they are treacherous. Harangued by her brother about the dangers of her relationship with Hamlet, forced by her father to return the prince's love tokens and foreswear any further contact with him, before being used as a pawn in the king's espionage, and then subjected to Hamlet's violent disgust and disgusting jokes, she too loses a father in unexplained and violent circumstances. But Shakespeare gives us virtually no sense of Ophelia as an interior self through the modes of self-expression that he affords the prince. Hamlet may contemptuously dismiss the desire to unpack one's heart with words as the mark of a whore, but Ophelia, whom he all but calls a whore more than once, shows no such inclination or capacity.

If Denmark is a prison for Hamlet, it is a torture chamber for Ophelia. Unlike the prince, Ophelia has no form of expression that might reserve an inner self for her authentic being. Whatever that interior being may be, we are never given any direct access to it. At a school workshop that I ran on *Hamlet*, girls and boys tended to be divided about Ophelia. The girls thought that Hamlet treats her abominably; the boys generally thought she was a wimp. To break this stand-off I encouraged them to stop thinking about either Hamlet and Ophelia as if they were one of their school friends, whom they are inclined to like or despise, avoid or befriend, and to think instead of them as expressions of the possibilities of certain kinds of action or passivity, determined by their place in a set of social and linguistic relationships: what kind of *I* is available to Ophelia, and how is that circumscribed or determined by its relation to the others of brother, father, king and princely lover? What can Ophelia think, feel or do, given these constraints?

My advice seemed to them to be a counter-intuitive way of looking at literary characters. But they seemed finally to accept that to look at Ophelia as the embodiment of a social system of possible ways of speaking offers us a view beyond individual character to the conditions that make such a character possible. That is to say, we try to recognize the historical distance of Hamlet's work from us in order to understand the social conditions that restrict or enable personal agency as the activity of language, the performance of available speech acts. Ophelia speaks, but in stark contrast to Hamlet, she says only what her predetermined social role allows her to say. This particular prison-house finally creates, as Foucault says of the modern prison, an image of Ophelia's soul, but only as an absence, as something *not* finally expressed from within its own interior being, in words that it can call its own: 'nothing'.

The language that Shakespeare gives Ophelia as a vehicle for self-expression is the language of madness. But rather than being inscrutably private it is conventional, impersonal and public. Her madness is not the antic disposition that Hamlet adopts to display brilliant wit and dazzling paradoxes. Hers is altogether more alienated and therefore strangely moving. After she has obeyed her father's command to return Hamlet's letters and tokens and see him no more, after being used as a spy in her father and the king's tawdry plots and subjected to Hamlet's violent rage and disgust, she returns to express the pain and desire she has been forced to suppress in the words of popular, bawdy songs and the mute, folk symbols of herbs and flowers:

> By Gis, and by Saint Charity,
> Alack, and fie for shame!
> Young men will do 't if they come to 't;
> By Cock, they are to blame.
> Quoth she 'Before you tumbled me,
> You promised me to wed',
> So would I 'a done, by yonder sun,
> An thou hadst not come to my bed'. (5.4.56–64)

In this, just one of the songs through which Ophelia speaks, the pronouns indicate the dislocation of her sense of self or the speaking *I*. She speaks of herself not in the first but rather in the third person, as *she*, and when she does occupy the first-person pronoun in the song it is as a persona suggestive of Hamlet: the faithless *male* seducer, who 'will do't if they come to it'.

If Hamlet has been admired and endlessly analysed for the profound, inner inscrutability of his soliloquies, Ophelia's personal voice is displaced, her soul conveyed through public forms rather than expressed in words that could be construed as her own. Only through the most exterior forms of popular expression, which circulate without personal attribution or authorship – that is to say, without being the expression of any single self or interiority – can Ophelia find a voice to convey her anger and pain. If song expresses a sustaining sense of solidarity against the coldness of the prison, it marks Ophelia's isolation and otherness in the prison of Denmark. Even in death she remains the disputed property of political and religious discourses that have shaped her during her life. Her death by drowning hovers undecidably between willed action and passive abjection. Men argue about the nature of her death; they come to blows over her as the instrument of their own sense of subjectivity; and the debate over the possibility or likelihood of her suicide means that she is given the scantest burial rites.

Three Women Prisoners Speak

There were no women on Robben Island. So we have no idea what a woman might have chosen from her reading, or recollection from school or university, of Shakespeare. I have discussed a particular discourse of subjected femininity that is discernible in the writing of Dlamini, noted Middleton's complaint that the Island had become in a broader post-Apartheid discourse, a simulacrum of *all* prison experience, and suggested analogies with the treatment of Ophelia in what her lover, Hamlet, perceives as the 'prison' of the Danish court in which she is trapped.

I now want to leave the Island to visit the representations of their detention by three different women: Ruth First (wife of the SA

Communist Party leader, Joe Slovo), who was subjected to solitary detention in a police station for some 4 months in the sixties, and subsequently assassinated with a letter bomb; Emma Mashanini, a trade unionist who was detained in solitary confinement without being charged, and Caesarina Makhoere, a young member of the 1976 generation, who was imprisoned with other black female political prisoners in Kroonstad Prison, about a hundred miles from where I grew up. What each of these women shows, in sometimes radically different ways, is the consequence of the stripping away of the ordinary that is exemplified especially by solitary confinement, and the impossibility of any retreat into an interior self.

In her memoir, *117 Days*, First represents the confinement of solitary detention as very different from the communal world of Robben Island. It is clear, from her opening sentence, that prison time and prison space are experienced together as peculiarly determinative and constricting. 'For the first fifty-six days of my detention in solitary,' First writes, 'I changed from a mainly vertical to a mainly horizontal creature. A black iron bedstead became my world.'[28] Given First's bourgeois lifestyle outside the police cell, the world she presents is not only severely constricted but also turned upside-down. The window, multiply barred and meshed, is 'a closing, not an opening', the 'naked electric bulb' burns as 'single yellow eye', the 'grey prison blankets were as heavy as tarpaulins, and smelt of mouldy potatoes' (9). First's description transforms the potentially domestic in the objects and spaces into the alienating and the oppressive. Yet, even in this opening description we learn of the powers of adaptation and transformation, even control and self-possession, on the most meagre of terrains: First 'learned to ignore the smell and to wriggle round the lumps on the mattress', and although she 'feared to become one of those colourless insects that slither under a world of flat, grey stones', feeling that the iron bedstead was 'like being closed inside a matchbox' (9), that shrunken world is soon transformed into a kind of 'room of one's own' by her withdrawal into an interior space which is in effect the real space of *117 Days*.

> Yet the bed was my privacy, my retreat, and could be my secret life. On the bed I felt in control of the cell. I did not need to survey it; I could ignore it, and concentrate on making myself comfortable. I could sleep, as long as I liked, without fear of interruption. I could think, without diversion, I could wait to see what happened, from the comfort of my bed. (9)

The world constituted by the 'black iron bedstead' is essentially an inner world, in which the horizontal passivity of the body is balanced by the activity of the mind. First almost seems to welcome the opportunity to be free of people and their impositions: she can think 'without diversion', 'concentrate on making myself comfortable', and, with the sense of control over her life that is the very antithesis of most detainees' experiences, sleep 'without fear of interruption' while choosing to ignore everything that constitutes the physical or material space around her in a new-found 'retreat' or 'secret life'. Fear, the quintessential emotion of the detainee, is reduced to the irritation of being imposed upon; comfort, hardly likely on a lumpy mattress smelling of mouldy potatoes, becomes a state of mind. The prison cell is a projection of First's fantasies beyond its walls of escaping from the uncomfortable and irritating pressures of other people, including her family: 'for as long as I could, I would draw satisfaction from the time I had, at last, to think! Uninterruptedly, undistracted by the demands of daily living and working' (18).

First thus encapsulates one of Hamlet's dreams: a retreat into 'that within' 'undistracted' by the demands of others or of the world outside. But it soon turns out to be a nightmare. Like Hamlet, she offers a highly developed representation of an interior self, which is not only able to withdraw from a threatening world, but also determined to present itself to that world (in the shape of the reader) as someone utterly disciplined and controlled. Confident at first that isolation will provide a much desired retreat from the public world, First soon realizes that 'isolation and privacy' are 'not the same thing by any means' (29). Both the sense of control that she projected from her 'secret retreat' in the opening page and her claimed relief from external interference are recognized as self-deceptive, and by the time she is transferred to Pretoria Central Prison – 'like being sealed in a sterile tank of glass in a defunct aquarium' – both the lack of human contact and the peculiar sterility of the new prison space begin to change her representation of time and self. First begins an extended description of the results of such a systematic and alienating 'dissociation from humanity': 'I was suspended in limbo, unknowing, unreached' (71). This sense of being in limbo drives the narrative inwards, into the interior spaces of reading, day-dreaming and self-reflection. Her early project of self-sustained and self-sustaining thought ('I . . . tried to shake myself into disciplined thinking') is now rendered much more difficult, and the novel that she attempts to write in her head is soon reduced to the constricting realities of her immediate condition. Like her memoir, it turns inward, becoming a means for 'getting behind' her characters, for exploring and 'dissecting' the very 'secret retreat' that First celebrated on her opening page. She finds the movement into interiority and memory not liberating and stabilizing, but rather increasingly disorienting: 'I put myself through self-scrutiny but in a scattered, disorganized fashion and I found myself not with clearer insight into myself in this abnormal situation, but with the diffused world of the past diverting me from the poverty of the present. I was appalled at the absence of my inventive and imaginative powers' (73).

First finally finds herself caught in an erotic flirtation with one of her interrogators, Lieutenant Viktor (whom we shall meet again in the next chapter). As their relationship develops he speaks to her as a knowing, indulgent and paternalistic lover: '"I will never lose my temper with you," Viktor told me repeatedly', and, more ominously, 'I know you better after a month than people who have known you your whole life' (137) and 'If you tell me anything it must be the truth, or I will know' (141). Of this dependency on her interrogator, First writes, 'I loathed myself but it seemed I could not resist taking part in this exchange with another human being, talking, responding, proving I was not a caricature, a prototype, but a person' (140). She believes at first that 'he was becoming a fascinating case study', but soon realizes that, despite his affable chatter about himself and expressions of concern for her, the power of the gaze belonged to him, not to her. She is especially exposed and vulnerable when Viktor begins to sit in on her visits from family and children, and her anxiety at his continuous presence, made all the worse for being apparently considerate and sympathetic, culminates in her inability to read a thriller with the forbidding title, *The Night of the Thousand Eyes*: 'for the first time in my life I was afraid of a book, because the thousand eyes of the title were the force of telepathy and I felt the eerie presence of Viktor's scrutiny at the back of my neck' (142). She attempts suicide, provoked by her sense of helpless entanglement after she begins to make a statement and realizes with horror that she has no hope of controlling the process: 'I was breaking down my own resistance. It was madness for me to think I could protect myself in a session like this, in any session with them. . . . I was open to emotional blackmail, and the black mailer was myself' (122, 127). The recognition that she was subjecting herself to emotional blackmail is both an acknowledgement of independent agency and her absolute dependency on the society of others, even if they were her jailers. Her intense scrutiny of herself leads her to the discovery that a perfectly interior life is not sustainable, and that in turn gives rise to intense feeling of guilt and self-flagellation. She feels guilty for being human.

Emma Mashinini's activism in the women's labour movement led to her detention in 1981 in Pretoria Central Prison: 'I was cold. Everything was taken . . . I sat in that place with nothing to read. Just with myself. The bare me.'[29] Isolation was a devastating experience, an especially unremitting, slow dribbling away of the self in the form of memory loss and paranoia, apathy and despair. Striking about Mashinini's experience, in contrast to First's, is the way in which the simulacra of domesticity in the prison are precisely what rob her of her sense of self. In contrast to First's foetid, uncomfortable police cell, and even the conditions on Robben Island, Mashinini's is inhumanely antispectic: 'The cell was a very small cell. There was a toilet, there was a basin to wash. The toilet was a proper flush toilet, very clean. Extremely clean' (61). Like First, however, Mashinini recognizes the degree to which isolation in which interminable periods of loneliness are broken only by the alternating hostility and humanity of the interrogators turns the self into its own instrument of destruction: 'These people have fine ways of torturing you. They let you torture yourself' (65). One of the worst instances of this self-torture is the terrible experience of forgetting her daughter's name:

> One day, thinking about my own children . . . thinking about their faces, and putting names to them, I could see my youngest daughter's face and I wanted to call her by her name. I struggled to call out the name, the name I always called her, and I just could not recall what the name was. I struggled and struggled. I would fall down and actually weep with the effort of remembering the name of my daughter. I'd try and sleep on it, wake up. I'd go without eating, because this pain of not being able to remember the name of my own daughter was the greatest I've ever had. And then, on the day when I actually did come across the name – this simple name Dudu, or "Love" – I immediately fell asleep, because it was such a great relief. But that was after days of killing myself to remember my own child's name. (86)

The self which is still reassuringly present after the first two weeks of empty waiting here dissolves in the very process of attempting to retain and re-enact the small rituals of normal community and intimacy. Mashinini's struggle is not merely to re-call but to 'call out the name' aloud, as if to make her daughter present. This crucial loss of memory is both a kind of death and a cause for the most intense self-affliction – 'killing myself to remember my own child's name'. We see in this passage the almost magical import of names for human beings. The 'simple' name, when it comes, is actually a very complex phenomenon. Its very simplicity signals everything that is contrary to the brutal conditions of her incarceration, both through its meaning, 'Love', and its signification of Mashinini's most intimate membership of human society, denied so systematically by the conditions of detention.

In her almost total deprivation of human company, Mashinini attempts to represent a sense of an enduring self, even if it is only to convey its deathly experiences. Absence, emptiness, nothing constitute the core of that experience to the extent that it is reflected as an interior space, even during the momentary (and paradoxical) relief of interrogation, when the police attempt to wrest the 'truth' from her: 'Always they wanted the truth, when I had no more truth to tell. I don't think they ever understood that in fact there was nothing to give away. But they always tried to find it, this nothing' (75). Few statements could capture so succinctly the curious, frightening relationship between interrogation and 'truth': not a manifold of real events waiting to be released into the present, but a fiction, a projection of interrogation itself upon the emptiness of the interrogated.

If First and Breytenbach experience the process of writing in interrogation as vertiginous loss of self and an inevitable slippage into betrayal, Mashinini sees this writing as a way of escaping the constant bullying control of her jailers, of regaining command over herself: 'I would sit and write, and write. And this was better for me. Maybe it was a way of being able to think what to say without for once anyone pushing me and going on – "Come on, come on, now. Speak." And being rough about it' (76). Unlike Breytenbach and First, Mashinini uses writing to externalize rather than internalize the self, thereby forging some sort of respite from interrogation from within it. This need to reflect the self off the world outside becomes signally apparent when she reflects on the sudden emptiness caused by the abrupt cessation of her interrogation sessions:

> That was it – bang. No word. Nothing about why. And I missed them. I thought once again I was going to be sitting in that room

> all by myself. I didn't think I knew myself any longer. *There was no mirror.* It's odd what happens to you when you don't see yourself in a mirror for such a long time. You don't recognize yourself. You think, who am I? All I had to recognize was a jersey which was sent to me by a friend. It was her jersey and I could recognize it. But I didn't know any longer how to recognize myself. (87; my emphasis)

In its poignant simplicity, this is beautifully put; it is the other side of her terrible loss of her daughter's name. In the balanced images of mirror and jersey, Mashinini touches on the social as the foundation of the self, crystallized in her native proverb, *Motho ke motho ka batho babang.*[30] Without a mirror, in effect, without other people, self-consciousness cannot be sustained. What does sustain Mashinini's sense of herself 'inside' are fragments from 'outside': her daughter's name; the chain from her daughters and her rings taken away when she is arrested; images of her husband and neighbourhood; writing of her trade union activities; and the jersey that negotiates a passage between these two 'spaces': hers and not hers, inside and outside, a token of friendship and support from beyond the walls.

Caesarena Kona Makhoere's *No Child's Play: In Prison under Apartheid* is the voice of a different generation, proclaiming in its title not only the harshness of imprisonment, but the putting aside, by one of the 'children of Soweto', of childish things.[31] Makhoere was detained on 25 October 1976, after her father, a policeman, had revealed her hiding place to the security police. She was interrogated, assaulted, tried and sentenced to 5 years' imprisonment on 27 October 1977, after a year in detention. (Had she been male, she would have been one of the unruly youths who challenged Mandela and his companions on Robben Island.) This year – 367 days, 250 days longer than First's detention – is represented in six pages.[32] The rest of the book, just over a hundred pages, is devoted to the 5 years she spent first in the women's section of the Kroonstad jail, then in Pretoria Central and Klerksdorp prisons (where Mandela's wife, Winnie, was imprisoned only a year earlier). Although Makhoere spent long periods of her time as a convicted prisoner either in isolation or in solitary confinement, her detention before her trial, like that of others, was entirely solitary. After her conviction she did have the company of fellow prisoners in both Kroonstad and Klerksdorp.

I emphasize this because it is indicative of the focus of her narrative, in which an interior self is almost entirely absent. Time, the very substance of the isolated and detained consciousness in other memoirs, is virtually absent in *No Child's Play*, which confines itself to the description of action, event and the unselfconscious expression of emotions and attitudes like anger, indignation, condemnation and self-assurance. If Mashinini seeks a stable, recognizable self without at times being assured of it, the issue doesn't arise for Makhoere, who simply acknowledges the limits of her ability to convey weakness and humiliation: 'The ordeal I went though still hurts today. Other people have described how helpless you feel, how at some point you no longer know you're human; that's how I felt' (8). Forced to try to describe the experience of confinement on a reduced diet in which even the windows are painted white to cut her off completely from the outside world, Makhoere's account is perfunctory, a mere catalogue of relatively abstract actions and mental states, time being counted by the very measures which First pronounces too crude to catch the slowness of its passing:

> There was nothing. Nothing. No bible. No reading material at all. I was there on my own. Twenty-three hours 30 minutes went by like this. I was taken for a bath. After the bath, exercise. Back in the cell. For the next 23 hours 30 minutes, speaking to myself, singing, laughing, growing paranoid, hallucinating. You think of all things.
>
> I got depressed. The anger, the hatred was building.

> It affected my mind. At about eight o'clock in the evening I would hear footsteps, and think, "These people are coming to kill me." It worked into my mind. (73)

At this most intense moment of solitariness, in which bodily stimulus and action are reduced absolutely, Makhoere uses the word 'mind' to donate some kind of interior locus of this torture, but is unable to sustain a properly developed representation of self-consciousness. The 'mind' of which she writes is removed, abstracted, a mere word, one might say, just as the second-person pronoun in 'you think of all things' renders the 'thinking' denoted even more general and impersonal.

One grasps well enough what she wants to convey about solitary detention, but there is neither an attempt to relive the experience nor the movement into self-exploration that this condition induces in First or Sachs, Lewin or Breytenbach. Dorothy Driver has remarked on the absence of what she calls 'self-doubt' in Makhoere's writing: 'In Makhoere's account generally, narrating and experiencing selves are rarely split, leaving no space for self-criticism or character development that autobiography and other first-person narration typically invite, and that Benson and Mashinini, to different degrees, employ' (350).[33] Driver goes on to say that Makhoere's exclusion of any space for an inquiry into the constructions of the self in her writing means that 'she remains "in prison under apartheid" . . . even when she is apparently free' (353).

It is difficult not to share Driver's unease with the relentlessly combative mode of *No Child's Play*, with its incorrigible presentation of a self given to total resistance, to 'say[ing] No at every turn' (Driver, 349). But Makhoere's refusal to 'torture herself' – to seek a retreat into an interiority that will turn out to be 'nothing' – forces us to review the notion that first-person narrative necessarily provokes self-criticism or character development, or that a first-person narrative without these qualities is intrinsically defective. Makhoere's narrative displays a finely nuanced grasp of the protocols and conventions of ordinary social intercourse, the absence of which is so disturbing to Mashinini. By refusing to make any complaints, register any requests or eat the food thrust at her, Makhoere refuses to acknowledge the people who treat her with systematic contempt as human beings; she refuses to share her humanity with them. This is a kind of resistance, although in Mashinini's case it leads to a loss of self, a collapse of a tenuous kind of interiority into the emptiness of the absent mirror or the fragile possession of a borrowed jersey.

Makhoere works through the public forms of language and behaviour that the historical development of the first-person narrative has taught us to see as mere outward signs of an inner condition. When she insists that the warders begin their own sentence with her, she is insisting on the fact that they are incorrigibly tied to her and her companions through complicated webs of social connections. Underlying this sense is an unshakeable conception of a moral order: of the imperative of mutual respect and equal treatment. Makhoere's strategy is never to allow her jailers to use these connections as a way of maintaining power over the prisoners: to insist that these connections be mutual, and that they can operate only under certain conditions:

> Captain Callitz and this fool Du Plessis began to take the line that: "You people are never satisfied. When we give you this you want something more. Every day. I've never heard you saying thank you." And then we would ask them, "What is there to thank you for? To thank you for imprisoning us? Then you must be joking. (36)

A jailer who expects thanks opens himself or herself up to the humanity of the other, to being rebuked by the withholding of thanks. This is what especially upsets Mashinini in prison: the complete lack of common courtesy, of the conditions which make courtesy possible, and it is in part what causes her debilitating withdrawal into herself. It is in the logic of thanks as a speech act that it cannot be demanded. Makhoere understands this perfectly well, turning it into a devastating source of moral power over her captors. When she refuses to stand at attention for inspection in the mornings it is because she is expected to smile a greeting during that inspection, and she balks, more than anything else, at the lack of mutuality in the greeting: 'That parading was disgusting, humiliating – how could they expect you to be polite to them while they continued to control your life, to control your everything?' (54). When Makhoere and her companions invent the 'dis' – to disregard the person speaking, as if they did not exist – as a weapon, they are collectively adopting Mashinini's refusal to treat verbal transactions with jailers as proper conversations, as interactions between human beings. The 'dis' is so powerful because it denies the humanity of the other, severing the contact that makes the exercise of power possible.

> Now we took a resolution that we were not going speak to them: they knew our position. They would come and we would ignore them. We called it 'dis', for 'disregard' – you 'dis', you give them 'dis'. That one weapon completely frustrated them, they became flustered. They did not know how to handle that. (52)

Makhoere's delight in this 'weapon' arises not only from its effectiveness, but also from the pleasure of their inventiveness, a creativity forged together and encapsulated in the relish with which she uses the coined word.

In its extensive concern with interiority, and through First's own considerable command over the representational conventions of time and space as processes of an essentially *inner* consciousness, *117 Days* conforms to the very 'technology of representation' upon which Foucault claims the modern art of punishment rests (104). The 'invention of the soul', which Foucault attributes to the birth of the modern prison, is reflected in relatively recent representational conventions by which 'the penitentiary is imagined as the meeting point of the individual mind and material causes'.[34] Unshaped by the sense of the soul that Foucault attributes to the penitentiary, and which John Bender argues is similarly constitutive of the rise of the first-person narrative as Driver describes it, the 'I' of Makhoere's narrative is differently signified than the 'I' of First's. Each 'I' brings different rewards, explores different terrains, is able to withstand different pressures and is liable to be complicit with very different structures.

The critical thing about the three women I have discussed is how radically different their representations of self and imprisonment are from the supposed exemplum of Robben Island. None of them has access to Shakespeare; none of them mentions him. But each, in very different ways, throws light on what it means both to be subject to a repressive society from which the possibilities of the ordinary have been removed, and to take arms against that society. Each reflects and refracts the possibilities and impossibilities of subjectivity that are apparent in the dance of Hamlet and Ophelia. If First and Mashinini represent the impossibility of retreating into a stable interior self that 'passes show', finding in the end, 'nothing', Makhoere offers a frightening picture of the prince as unreflecting man of action, in which the self is subsumed as pure, resisting performance.

Conclusion

Where has my argument taken us? First, if it is correct to claim that Shakespeare invents or discovers a way of representing human interiority in the character of Hamlet, then it is precisely Hamlet's experience of Denmark as a prison that produces this sense of a supposedly *real*, inner self. The prison calls the self into being. Second, recalling Dlamini's thoughtless declaration of what properly belongs to the part of woman or the essence of femininity and my discussion of

First, Mashinini and Makhoere, we recognize that, like Middleton's male prisoners in the SABC interview, Hamlet's representation of selfhood is hardly representative.

We have seen that Hamlet tries to find a refuge for his own sense of being 'out of joint' with the time in Denmark by withdrawing into an isolated, and ultimately inexpressible, inner self. But such interiority is a place of nightmares – it is precisely what prevents him from 'counting himself the king of infinite space'. Taking refuge inside oneself under these circumstances is the equivalent of placing oneself in solitary confinement to escape the restrictions of the prison. The opposite position, of being both exposed to and wholly determined by a predetermined social role, is no less intolerable. Ophelia's plight is echoed by a female sonneteer and contemporary of Shakespeare, Lady Mary Wroth, who writes of her position in the court of James I as one of tortured exposure to the public eye:

> . . . look on me; . . .
> I am the soul that feels the greatest smart:
> I am that heartless Trunk of hearts depart;
> And I that One, by love, and grief oppressed . . .
> I should not have been made this Stage of woe,
> Where sad Disasters have their open show . . .[35]

Wroth's social imprisonment involves the painful exposure – the stripping – of which Lewin writes: of being made a stage of woe, a heartless torso tortured not only by love, the loss of her heart, but also by the gendered prohibitions on desire and love.

In general, then, Hamlet's Denmark, like the court of James for Wroth, is a prison because it imposes upon everyone the relentless scrutiny of a public gaze. This is not to say that Shakespeare's play anachronistically calls for a withdrawal into a secure private world untouched by the public or political realm. Rather, *Hamlet* reveals the political nature of even the most private relations; the stories I have been able to tell around the Robben Island Shakespeare reveal the indispensability of the private within the institution that most relentlessly seeks to destroy it. Both *Hamlet* and the writings from 'inside' call for space to be provided for the ordinary – for personal relations in a healthy polis. The political tensions between the private and the public exist in every society, but they are rendered especially starkly in conditions such as are represented in *Hamlet* or the experience of prison in the modern world.

Just as we see these tensions in the woman poet, Mary Wroth, so we can also recognize the world of Hamlet in the more intimate or personal realm of Shakespeare's sonnets. Sonnet 125 is the penultimate poem addressed to the famous 'fair friend', the aristocratic youth who may have been Shakespeare's patron, and probably, for a while at least, his lover. It is a plea to be allowed to escape a certain *kind* of politics, if not politics as such: it seeks to withdraw from the politics of outward show, but without discovering a *real* interiority. The canopy that the poet refers to in the opening lines is a metaphor for his own poetry as a form of praise and allegiance declared publicly to a socially elevated beloved. The sonnet tries to negotiate the declaration of love within a social space filled with 'pitiful thrivers' – competitors whose declarations of allegiance are calculated to maximize personal profit:

Were 't aught to me I bore the canopy,
With my extern the outward honouring,
Or laid great bases for eternity
Which proves more short than waste or ruining?
Have I not seen dwellers on form and favour
Lose all, and more, by paying too much rent,
For compound sweet forgoing simple savour –
Pitiful thrivers, in their gazing spent?
No, let me be obsequious in thy heart,
And take thou my oblation, poor but free,
Which is not mix'd with seconds, knows no art

> But mutual render, only me for thee.
> Hence, thou suborned informer! A true soul
> When most impeach'd, stands least in thy control.

The poem is a small piece of theatre; it is addressed by a lover, friend or servant (or a combination of all three) to a social superior as a plea to withdraw, like Hamlet, from a world of seeming and show; it attacks the public theatricality of expected devotion and asks instead for a mutuality of the heart that, 'poor but free', transcends the profitless sycophancy (the 'pitiful thrivers') of a corrupt public world. But like Ophelia, like Hamlet, like Mary Wroth, like the prisoner, the final two lines discover that space of withdrawal has already been invaded and occupied by someone else: the suborned spy, the lurking informer. Stripped to its absolute essence, this sonnet tries to unpack its poet's heart in a mutual exchange of the self as a gift, but finds the personal space into which it tries to withdraw already occupied by another. Its poignancy lies in its recognition of the contradictions we have seen in *Hamlet*: between the competing worlds of private devotion and the public spaces in which such devotion has to be declared and lived. It pleads for the suspension of a certain kind of debilitating politics while recognizing that the very condition of possibility of its withdrawal is the polis in general, the community of human beings that make both language and love possible. That problem, which is the problem of friendship and trust, is the subject of the next chapter.

The writers who sought to give expression to the integrity and intensity of their interior lives in the face of structural tyranny and confinement in the South African prison memoir were probably not aware of the role that Shakespeare played in the historical development of such representation. But by signing their names against passages in the book that bore Shakespeare's name, they appropriated Shakespeare's voice as their own – they crossed the *I* of his writing with their own. In doing so they achieved a collective expression of the self in the prison of which Hamlet can only dream. What

Hamlet does not see – and what escapes us too, and possibly some of those who crossed Shakespeare's dramatic voices with their own – is the degree to which his own actions contribute to the violation of people he believes he loves. Shakespeare reveals that unconscious violation both in its specificity and its general, structural conditions. He shows us trapped in language that is not our own creation, but at the same time he reveals our complicity as agents who, finding our place in the house of language, are free either to accommodate or exclude other people.

When we watch or read a play like *Hamlet* we are challenged to accept our own responsibility for the kind of interaction that makes language and human community possible. Shakespeare asks us to confront both the isolation of our subjection to what is often called the prison-house of language and to accept the degree to which our particular conceptions of community may constitute a prison for those whom, often without thought, we alienate as 'others', the 'theys', 'thems', 'hes', 'shes' – often, appallingly, as 'its' – that are the grammatical conditions both of Apartheid as prison and of our own identities. They are the necessary counterparts of our capacity to say 'I'. *We* are Hamlet's dreams.

Chapter 3
Friendship and Struggle

In his explanation of his choice of the passage from *Hamlet* from the Robben Island Bible, Saths Cooper reflects on the 'falling off' of the values of the struggle against Apartheid in the 'new' South Africa. Whereas Mandela chose Caesar's suitably pithy expression of the virtues of political courage ('Cowards die many times before their deaths: / The valiant never taste of death but once' (*Julius Caesar*, 2.2.32–3)), the contrary, youthful Black Consciousness leader selected a more enigmatic speech, in which Hamlet reflects on the nature of custom and the drinking habits of his despised uncle.

This heavy-headed revel east and west
Makes us traduc'd and tax'd of other nations;
They clepe us drunkards, and with swinish phrase
Soil our addition; and, indeed, it takes
From our achievements, though perform'd at height,
The pith and marrow of our attribute.
So, oft it chances in particular men
That, for some vicious mole of nature in them,
As in their birth, wherein they are not guilty,
Since nature cannot choose his origin;
By the o'ergrowth of some complexion,
Oft breaking down the pales and forts of reason;
Or by some habit that too much o'erleavens
The form of plausive manners – that these men,
Carrying, I say, the stamp of one defect,

> Being nature's livery or fortune's star,
> His virtues else be they as pure as grace,
> As infinite as man may undergo,
> Shall in the general censure take corruption
> From that particular fault. The dram of eale
> Doth all the noble substance of a doubt
> To his own scandal. (*Hamlet*, 1.3.17–38)

In part, Cooper tells us, he was attracted to this speech because many of the most famous speeches had already been chosen; in part because he wished to avoid hackneyed quotations; but mostly because it seemed to him – then, on Robben Island, in the midst of the struggle – to characterize the inevitable corruption of human beings, exemplified by what he terms 'the duplicity, the playing of different kinds of roles' and the 'crass power, personalized aggrandizement and everything that is corrupt in human nature that makes us part of the rest of the world' (Hahn interview, 5 February 2008; also Desai 23–4). No Robben Island exceptionalism here.

Cooper is one of the very few prisoners who refuses to romanticize the Island as the centre of solidarity and comradeship: the so-called University from which all graduated in united opposition to the regime. Instead he insists that 'the hardships, the frailties, the sheer dehumanization that you had to confront . . . brought out often the worst in us than the best' (Hahn). More than 30 years after he had marked Hamlet's disillusioned reflection on both the new king and the Danish character, Cooper decries the general 'cynicism' among young South Africans that is 'the legacy of leadership that has tended to look after itself, has tended to look after those that are close to them and then created a terrible model for the youth to follow'.

In her interview in Jenny Schreiner's collection, Barbara Hogan, who became Minister of Health and Minister of Public Enterprises in Jacob Zuma's cabinet from September 2008 to October 2010, reflects on the fact that all institutions concerned with power are open to abuse and corruption. She learned this first-hand, she says, from the 'closed community' of the prison:

> A closed community. You stand out in that community and you've betrayed them . . . If you are going to get anywhere you play the line. And every wardress spies on the other wardresses . . . What created my personal crisis was that I was saying to myself if it was so simple for evil to emerge out of an institution [like the prison], what right have we, say in the ANC, to say that we can guarantee that institutions which we create won't be of a similar kind. Institutions are all-powerful organizations. I began thinking that no matter what cause you fight, the good and the bad can fight the right, and the good and the bad can fight the wrong cause as well . . . And the corruption of power, and how power can corrupt individuals, institutions. With too much power and no counterbalancing forces there is nothing to stop corruption from saturating the system.[1]

The striking phrase in Hogan's reflection on the fact that all institutions – including the one to which she had committed her political life – are open to corruption, is 'a closed community'. The community forged on Robben Island was closed. Not simply because it was enclosed by external forces and material barriers, but because, pressured by those forces, it forged both a reactive and creative sense of its own cohesiveness. The Robben Island Shakespeare is merely one small text in the weft and weave of this process. All the representations of life on the island begin with the forging of a closed community within an all-powerful institution that sought to forestall that process at every structural level. If we return to a classical conception of community – a polis – then it takes as its basis, from Aristotle to Cicero – the ideal of friendship.

Friends

In Cooper's speech from Shakespeare's play, Hamlet is speaking to his friend, Horatio, who is the only person with whom he feels comfortable in the suffocating 'prison' of Denmark, and the only person he can trust. It is easy to overlook the fact that while *Hamlet* is the period's most complex example of revenge tragedy, it is also a study in the Renaissance and Classical concept of friendship; or perhaps more accurately, it is a representation of the limits of such a concept of friendship. For the play's protagonist at least, friendship is essentially located elsewhere, in Wittenberg rather than Elsinore. Horatio moves between these two worlds: from the easy, somewhat egalitarian camaraderie of the Protestant university to the closed, hierarchical institution of the Danish court, where affable royal rhetoric obscures not only dark deeds but also a society organized around diplomatic subterfuge and a system of intelligencing or spying. It is a world in which friends are set to wangle secrets from each other, fathers systematically seek to pluck out the heart of their sons' mystery, and use their daughters as decoys.[2]

The critical thing about Horatio and Hamlet's friendship is that it is out of place: it is displaced from an arena in which it is made possible into one where it cannot be sustained, at least in its ideal lineaments.[3] Their initial meeting represents Hamlet's surprise at seeing his university friend in the unaccustomed confines of his uncle's court, but it also registers Horatio's guarded, deferential manner in the new confines of Denmark:

> *Enter,* HORATIO, MARCELLUS, *and* BARNARDO.
> *Hor.* Hail to your lordship!
> *Ham.* I am glad to see you well.
> Horatio – or I do forget myself.
> *Hor.* The same, my lord, and your poor servant ever.
> *Ham.* Sir, my good friend. I'll change that name with you.
> (1.2.161–3)

In Elsinore Horatio insists upon his literal status as the prince's servant, but Hamlet turns that around, pointing out that as Horatio's friend, he in fact serves Horatio. Hamlet is trading on a classical conception of friendship, whereby friends are necessarily equals.[4] But the play itself continuously undercuts the prince's desire to 'change names' with Horatio. Horatio maintains his deferential respectfulness throughout, and though he supports Hamlet, there is no sense of the two of them being 'one soul in two bodies', as the ideal friendship between males was celebrated.[5] Hamlet's expression of admiration for his friend underlines another aspect of classical amity – the incorruptible virtue of the friend:

> *Ham.* Horatio, thou art e'en as just a man
> As e'er my conversation cop'd withal.
> *Hor.* O my dear lord !
> *Ham.* Nay, do not think I flatter ;
> For what advancement may I hope from thee,
> That no revenue hast but thy good spirits
> To clothe and feed thee? . . .
> Since my dear soul was mistress of her choice
> And could of men distinguish her election,
> Sh' hath sealed thee for herself ; for thou hast been
> As one, in suff'ring all, that suffers nothing;
> A man that Fortune's buffets and rewards
> Hast ta'en with equal thanks; and blessed are those
> Whose blood and judgement are so well commeddled
> That they are not a pipe for Fortune's finger
> To sound what stop she please. Give me that man
> That is not passion's slave, and I will wear him
> In my heart's core, ay, in my heart of heart,
> As I do thee. – Something too much of this. (3.2.52–72)

The qualities that Hamlet celebrates are those of free choice together with virtues in the friend that are nothing if not conventional: being 'just' and maintaining a firm disposition towards a Stoic self-control and reliability. Horatio is somebody who, in 'suffering all . . . suffers nothing'; who faces the difficulties of the world with courage and integrity; and who holds a perfect balance between passion or emotion and reason.

It is not clear that *Hamlet* as a whole fully endorses its prince's conception of Stoic friendship. Hamlet himself hardly lives up to the precepts of strict control over the passions and self-sufficient removal from, or at least imperviousness to, the world that he praises in Horatio; nor does their friendship constitute an independent mode of resisting the dark world of Elsinore. Hamlet consults his friend, shares his perceptions of events and confesses his feeling and thoughts to him, but he acts and dies alone. In the end he prevents Horatio from resorting to the 'felicity' of suicide, and burdens him with telling his story within a highly insecure, 'new' Denmark, now in the hands of an unstable militarist. In brief, Hamlet and Horatio's friendship – displaced from the possible egalitarianism of the university – does not seem to offer the basis for an ideal polity for which it was repeatedly celebrated by its classical and Renaissance proponents.[6]

It is, however, to be sharply contrasted with Hamlet's relationship with his other university acquaintances, Rosencrantz and Guildenstern, who are happy to be 'pipe[s] for Fortune's finger'. They are ready instruments of the king's courtly panopticon, and happily put on a show of easy, disinterested friendship to serve political power. Such a conception of friendship was the more prevalent one within the society for which Shakespeare wrote his play. To be a 'friend' in that sense did not mean having a deeply intimate bond with a man whom one would 'wear in [one's] heart's core', but rather being a member of a social network through which one could call upon the other for support, financial and political, in mutually reciprocal ways. Such friendship was, in Aristotle's terms, based on economic and political usefulness rather than the prime qualities of affection, virtue, equality and free choice. Friends in this anti-Aristotelian sense were complementary cogs in the social and economic machinery. As Colette Gordon succinctly puts it: 'To be friendless in early Modern England was to be without recourse to aid; more broadly . . . it was to be excluded from the economy.'[7]

I want to pursue the issue of friendship that is raised in Cooper's choice from *Hamlet* along two lines. First, despite the prominence of the Robben Island Shakespeare as an instrument and register of community, it is striking not only that none of the passages chosen is concerned with friendship as such, but also that friendship and friends do not play a central part in the accounts of life on the Island. Friends are mentioned, friendship is invoked, but in a general, fairly vague sort of way: no one provides access to specific, deep friendships on the island – the sharing of souls.[8] That is not to say that people on the island did not have close friendships; merely that the discourse of such close relationships does not play a major role in subsequent representations – it is displaced by a more overriding language of solidarity and general community. Second, I want to use the early modern alignment of friendship and credit to move beyond the Island into the world for which many saw it as a crucial form of preparation: for the new South Africa beyond Aparthcid, and its own, peculiar forms of friendship.

Cooper remarks that the speech he chose from *Hamlet* brought to mind 'the legacy of a leadership that looks after itself'. Implicit in his statement is the charge that the growing culture of corruption in the new South Africa had its *roots* (at least in part) in the Robben Island prison community – that, contrary to the traditional story of political growth and selfless community, the friendships of credit that took root after 1994 were not an aberration, but rather an inevitable outflow of prison conditions.[9]

A 'generally corrupt relationship'

Cooper doesn't mention any names, but to many in 2008 when the interview took place, the leadership that looks after itself and those close to them would have brought to mind the *locus classicus* of such behaviour (which appears now to be the norm rather than the exception): the 'generally corrupt relationship', in the words of Justice Hilary Squires, of Jacob Zuma and his friend, Schabir Shaik. Jacob Zuma was one of Cooper's fellow prisoners on Robben Island, a beneficiary of the Island's codes of unshakeable comradeship and sustaining education, a man moulded not only in the struggle, but also by the culture of friendship fostered through the hardships of incarceration. When Cooper reminds us of the other story, seldom mentioned in memoirs and reflection, of discord and violence, hypocrisy and nepotism on Robben Island itself, he puts pressure on the very idea of the comrade or the friend that emerges from the political history of the prison in particular and the struggle more generally. It is not clear whether Cooper would regard the corruption of human relationships as a general fault, or a 'vicious mole of nature' in specific men, but he certainly seems to view the present culture of self-serving nepotism as having grown out of the dehumanized conditions of Robben Island and the 'rotten state' as he puts it, of Apartheid South Africa itself.

Since Cooper made those remarks, the issue of corruption, of looking after oneself and one's own and the vicious falling out among thieves that ensues, has grown to what appear to many to be epidemic proportions.[10] Jacob Zuma, under suspicion for taking bribes as part of the notorious 'arms deal' (in which the newly elected ANC government bought, as virtually their first action in power, billions of Rands worth of arms from Western countries like Sweden, the United Kingdom and Germany), has been president of the country for 4 years, as a result of a palace revolt against his predecessor, Thabo Mbeki. Zuma has in turn had to expel the militant youth leader of the ANC Youth League, Julius Malema, who, after helping to bring him to power, turned against him.[11] In the process, Mac Maharaj, one of the major figures on Robben Island and the signatory of the speech from *Richard II* – 'Where words are scarce, they are seldom spent in vain; / For they breathe truth that breathe their words in pain' (2.1.7–8) – has himself come under suspicion, and has used all the powers at his command to suppress publication of his alleged corrupt behaviour.[12] (Maharaj is currently President Zuma's personal spokeman.) Robbed of the political and economic powers of patronage that his former position brought him, Malema is now under investigation for corruption.

Events are moving so fast as I write, at the beginning of 2012, that I cannot hope to cover them in the static format of a monograph. I shall therefore take the peculiar friendship between the newly elected Vice President of the ANC, Jacob Zuma, and his financial advisor, Schabir Shaik, as a paradigm case of the tendency to be 'traduc'd' that Cooper highlights.

'Reciprocal altruism'

After months of uncertainty, in 2006 Shaik was finally prosecuted for securing bribes for his client and friend, Zuma, from European arms manufacturers, and sentenced to a 15-year prison term for having a 'generally corrupt relationship' with Zuma. Thabo Mbeki immediately relieved Zuma of the position of Vice President, and for the better part of 2 years South Africans waited in suspense to see whether Zuma would also be prosecuted. The prosecuting authorities, under enormous political pressure, finally decided not to do so, and after a separate trial in which he was found not guilty of raping the daughter of a family friend, Zuma mobilized his friends to depose the man who had sacked him.

In the initial preparation of Schabir Shaik's appeal against Hilary Squires's sentence for his 'generally corrupt' relationship with Zuma, his lawyers intended to argue that that relationship was anything but corrupt. Instead, they attested, a friendship of a special kind existed between Shaik and Zuma, which had been forged in the comradeship of the struggle. The concept of such friendship, they argued, unfortunately received no legal recognition in a Western system essentially foreign to such affective relations. They called this relationship 'reciprocal altruism'.[13] Mo Shaik, Schabir's brother, put it this way: 'Our law does not have the language to deal with the reality of the transitional period. Regrettably we couldn't bring this to bear on the consciousness of the (trial) court.'[14] These conceptual grounds of appeal were changed in the end, but they were an attempt to invoke a concept that has a long history, traceable through Shakespeare, Montaigne and Cicero back to Aristotle.

This special kind of friendship went unrecognized, Shaik argued, by a legal system blind to the quality of the relationships forged during the struggle against Apartheid and endemic to an indigenous cultural system which recognized the essential dependency of people tied by far-reaching social and personal relationships. Indeed, throughout the initial trial Shaik had claimed that he could not be charged with bribing Zuma, because friends are conceptually incapable of suborning each other. They may help each other, shower each other with gifts; they cannot extort or corrupt each other through such gifts. A long tradition holds that they are one soul in two bodies. Montaigne argues that friends are in fact incapable even of giving each other anything, since a gift implies division and difference, and friends are the union of souls. The concept of 'reciprocal altruism' does not go that far: it retains the notion that the friends are separate beings, but it underscores a virtuous generosity shared equally and freely between them.

I do not want to revive the question of guilt, or seek to rehabilitate any specific character in this saga. I'm interested instead in the conceptual point – the friendship of a special type, 'reciprocal altruism' – its relation to Shakespeare, and the social and personal circumstances on Robben Island where the notion of comradely friendship had its most striking symbolic expression.

No one who signed the Venkatrathnam's Shakespeare marked anything from the *Henry IV* plays.[15] If we are looking for a representation of the political complexities of friendship and corruption, then the relationship between Falstaff and the heir apparent,

Prince Hal, is obvious. Zuma did not get to sign the Robben Island Shakespeare, because he was in one of the communal cells rather than in B section. But imagine that he had been asked to do so, and in the week or so that the book was with him, he had decided to read the second Henriad. What would he have learnt from the plays? What passage might he have marked for special notice, for its resonance with present times, since these two plays exemplify what Cooper calls 'the duplicity, the playing of different kinds of roles . . . crass power, personalized aggrandizement and everything that is corrupt in human nature' (Hahn interview)? They subject the problem of friendship to especially interesting scrutiny, and they reveal a historical shift in the concept that has striking parallels with the Shaik/Zuma relationship.

The question of the friendships of politics and the politics of friendship appears in these plays in a variety of forms. It is obvious in the parallel between the invocation of friendship among the rebels, both as the cement of their cause and as the reason for their insurrection. But it is developed in intricately complex ways in the companionship shared by the heir to the throne, Prince Hal, his friend, Sir John Falstaff, and the low-life, high-living gang which moves between the indulgences of the tavern and the opportunities of the highway.

Let's begin with the place of friendship in the rebellion. For the insurrection marks a conceptual shift in the position of the king vis-à-vis the possibilities and responsibilities of amity. In his justification of the rebellion, Worcester accuses Henry of forgetting and demeaning the obligations of friendship: for having turned his face against his friends, who helped him to the throne against the previous king. Henry IV thus exemplifies the condition of the feudal king who was the first among equals rather than the monarch as he or she was conceived in the royal universe established by the Tudors: a figure 'elevated . . . unapproachably above even the greatest of their lords'.[16] Worcester complains to his companions that the king 'doth begin / To make us strangers to his looks of love' (1.3.289–90) and reminds Henry directly that 'we were the first and dearest of your friends' (5.1.33). Laurie Shannon argues persuasively that the second Henriad is a study of the historical withdrawal of the royal body from the very possibility of friendship. The serial reflections of both Henry IV and V on the care and isolation of the king as such signal the transformation of the monarch from the 'first and dearest friend' to someone who would betray his duty to the commonwealth by dedicating himself to the kind of specially chosen, privileged companion celebrated by the classical discourse of friendship.

The striking thing about the friendship evoked by the rebels is that it need involve no affection. Such friendship or 'love' – a word invoked frequently – arises from a mutual need for security and protection rather than any depth of feeling or intimacy: a network of mutually beneficial relationships. It could be argued that among Robben Island prisoners, relationships of solidarity, support and community were similarly free of the *necessity* of intense affect. There may indeed have been close friendships, and it is clear that virtually everyone had a great deal of affection for Walter Sisulu, but the notion of the intensely intimate sharing of souls definitive of Montaigne's *amity* was displaced by a different discourse – a shared ideological and political commitment, based on resistance to a common enemy. Solidarity, not friendship, is the watchword of such relationships. Such relative independence of emotional ties with his comrades enabled Mandela to act independently of them in his decision to negotiate with the South African government on his own. There is no one with whom Mandela *feels the need* to share his thoughts or feelings beyond his general sense of loyalty to the cause. In the 1980s he was removed from the Island and most of his comrades, and put in a position to begin negotiation, on his own, with the government:

> I was now in a kind of splendid isolation . . . I chose to tell no one what I was about to do. Not my colleagues upstairs nor those in Lusaka . . . I knew that my colleagues upstairs would condemn

> my proposal and that would kill any initiative before it was born. There are times when a leader must move out ahead of the flock, go off in a new direction, confident that he is leading his people the right way. (*Long Walk*, 627)

Although Prince Hal raises issues of leadership that are not dissimilar from Mandela's, his relationship with Falstaff is contrasted with Mandela's unemotional analysis of his position insofar as an at least professed affection exists between Falstaff and Hal. I say that it is 'professed' because the degree to which Hal uses his friendship in his Machiavellian plot to emerge resplendent from his dissolute life among his tavern companions is not absolutely clear. Hal certainly seems to have some degree of love for his fat knight, and Falstaff affirms his strong affective bond with the prince, but their relationship would not have satisfied Aristotle's criteria of true friendship.

Their relationship disqualifies itself from such a noble status first because of the disparity between the prince and the knight. Socially they are unequal partners, and this dissimilarity is the object of much satirical commentary in a play that goes out of its way to contrast their sizes: the thin 'bull's pizzle' either overwhelmed by or penetrating and deflating the 'Mannigtree ox' (*1 Henry IV*, 2.4.238, 439). Following Aristotle further, the friendship is disqualified by its distinct lack of civic virtue. Friendship in the classical tradition is as much a public as a private relationship; consisting of an autonomous recognition of mutual virtue between free and equal agents, confined to men; it constitutes the fabric of a proper civic order – of what is 'just'. Montaigne follows this tradition only in part. His insistence that one can give no reasons for one's attachment to one's friend moves friendship into a realm in which the mutual recognition of virtue as the effective and affective cause of the relationship is excluded: 'If you press me to say why I loved him [Étienne de La Boétie]', he declares, 'I feel it cannot be expressed except by replying: "Because it was him, because it was me"' (Montaigne, *Essays*, 212). This means that there is no fundamental reason why Falstaff and

Hal should not be able to be soul mates. Nor should Jacob Zuma and Schabir Shaik in theory lack the capacity for a relationship characterized by 'reciprocal altruism'.

A scene usually celebrated for its evocation of a 'merry England' nostalgically recalled for its old-fashioned hospitality and rustic simplicity at the end of the second *Henry IV*, offers a further variation on friendship and its involvement with master–servant relations. Justice Shallow discusses domestic arrangements with his steward, Davy. The conversation encompasses the complex world of obligation and service, recompense and reprimand. There is plenty of reciprocity, but it is hardly selfless. Careless household servants are punished on the one hand, while Sir John and his minions are lavishly feasted, on the other, because, in a phrase of wonderfully expedient calculation, a 'friend i' th' court is better than a penny in purse' (5.1.29–30). Falstaff's men are to be 'used well' not for the sake of generous conviviality, but rather because they are 'arrant knaves, and will backbite' (32). The most significant moment in this scene, however, is the steward Davey's request that the justice 'countenance' his 'good friend' William Visor: that is to say, that he let him off the hook in the public world of the assize courts. To the master's rebuttal that Visor is no more than an 'arrant knave', Davy responds with the language of reciprocal self-interest:

> I grant your worship that he is a knave, sir; but yet, God forbid, sir but a knave should have some countenance at his friend's request. An honest man, sir, is able to speak for himself, when a knave is not. I have serv'd your worship truly, sir, this eight years; an I cannot once or twice in a quarter bear out a knave against an honest man, I have but a very little credit with your worship. The knave is mine honest friend, sir; therefore, I beseech you, let him be countenanc'd. (40–9)

This speech is not without satirical overtones, but it does register a set of real and settled social and personal conditions that, if not exactly altruistic, are certainly reciprocal, and moreover, in which the expectations of friendship are interwoven with the mutual obligations of master and servant. Davy can intercede on behalf of his 'honest friend' (who is in truth an 'arrant knave') with his master because of his 'credit' built up through 8 years of true service. What is more, such credit allows him to call continually upon his master: 'once or twice in a quarter'. Given that credit, it is enough for Davy to give no more reason than the mere fact of his 'honest friendship' and loyal service. Indeed, Shallow is himself aiming to establish an 'honest friendship' with the knavish knight, in the hope that he will be countenanced when Sir John's 'honest friend', the Prince of Wales, becomes king.

That Shallow's money has been lent in vain, his hospitality fallen on barren ground, is clear from Falstaff's derisory commentary after the meal, in which he ironically remarks on the degree to which master and servants have become the mirror images of each other:

> It is a wonderful thing to see the semblable coherence of his men's spirits and his. They, by observing him, do bear themselves like foolish justices: he, by conversing with them, is turned into a justice-like serving-man. Their spirits are so married in conjunction with the participation of society that they flock together in consent, like so many wild geese. If I had a suit to Master Shallow, I would humour his men with the imputation of being near their master; if to his men, I would curry with Master Shallow that no man could better command his servants . . . I will devise matter enough out of this Shallow to keep Prince Harry in continual laughter the wearing out of six fashions, which is four terms, or two actions, and a' shall laugh without intervallums. (5.1.55–87)

Shakespeare cannily gives the discourse of service exemplified by Davy and Shallow its full weight, but he also parodies it almost immediately, in the unlikely and ironical figure of Falstaff, himself both master and servant. For if the discourse of friendship posits an ideal of similarity between friends, Falstaff, himself an utterly corrupt master and conniving servant, suggests the levelling effects of the reciprocal nepotism that mark the general relation between master and servant. But his easy assumption that his satirical observations would make good matter for entertaining the Prince points to his own presumed credit with, and difference from, his master. There may be no 'semblable coherence' between the fat knight and the slender prince, but Falstaff nonetheless assumes that what he earlier invokes as his doing 'the part of a careful friend and a true subject' (2 *Henry IV*, 2.4.310) will allow him to laugh out the actions that the Chief Justice seeks against him, and he will have curried much greater favour with the future king than what can be achieved between master and servants in the Shallow household.

In the very next scene Hal, now Henry V, confronts the Chief Justice who, while fearful of what the new king might do to him in the light of his earlier treatment of him as reprobate Prince of Wales, recalls the doctrine of the king's two bodies that Falstaff's eager anticipation of keeping 'Harry in continual laughter' is apt to forget.[17] If the king's material body is prone to the pleasures and temptations of reciprocal altruism, the abstract body in whose name the Chief Justice acts when he disciplines even the heir apparent is alien to such affective reciprocity:

I then did use the person of your father;
The image of his power lay then in me;
And in th' administration of his law,
Whiles I was busy for the commonwealth,
Your highness pleased to forget my place,
The majesty and power of law and justice,
The image of the King whom I presented,
And struck me in my very seat of judgement;
Whereon, as an offender to your father,
I gave bold way to my authority
And did commit you. (5.2.73–82)

This body is transferable, from king to officer, so that Hal's striking the king's officer is in effect an act of raising his hand to the king, his father. The judge acts in the name or the place of the king when he exercises his authority over the prince. Note how closely the classical discourse of friendship approaches a doctrine that makes it impossible for the king to have friends: the Chief Justice and king are in effect one soul in two bodies, just as friends are meant to be, but it is the single soul of power and authority, in which affect as such can play no part. Falstaff assumes because he is the king's friend that authority and power will extend to *him*, and he expresses this thought in the most chilling line in the play – his triumphant cry as he speeds towards his monarch friend: 'Let us take any man's horse – the laws of England are at my commandment' (5.3.135–6). That largesse extends outwards, to encompass a whole set of relationships that are conceptually separate from Montaigne's notion of sovereign amity: 'Blessed are they that have been my friends,' Falstaff, continues, adding ominously, 'and woe to my Lord Chief Justice' (137–8). We know from the previous scene (though Falstaff doesn't) that Henry has now placed himself beyond both the kind of friendship and the aggressive settling of scores that such a relationship between sovereign and vassal – what Shannon calls *mignonerie* – implies.

Does Falstaff have a 'generally corrupt relationship' with Hal? Are Davy's expectations of reciprocal obligation implied by his service to his master and his 'honest friendship' with an 'arrant knave' corrupt? There is no universal answer to such questions. The second Henriad contains a relatively clear shift in the early modern possibilities of friendship within the sphere of politics and public life. Shakespeare presents a sufficiently engaging representation of the pleasures of friendship in the tavern and reciprocal obligations in master–servant relationships as a whole for us to feel something of the appeal and perhaps the historical and social appropriateness of what we would now call corrupt friendship. Falstaff is as much an attractive as a frightening figure of such friendship. But Shakespeare also registers the imperatives of a shift from feudal bonds of shared personal interests and animosities to the separation of justice and power from the natural body of the king, who becomes a figure distributed across others only in a wholly dispassionate, disinterested way, for the good or service of all. For such a king, the uneasiness that the crown brings cannot be disburdened by the shared affections or even relatively detached expectations of friendship. The king is necessarily beyond all forms of friendship. But that shift had not yet occurred when Henry V had to cope with the divisions in the country caused by his father's perceived ingratitude to the friends (his peers) who had helped him to the throne. Shakespeare is writing very much with hindsight, projecting the change in the concept of friendship backwards onto an early Lancastrian reign.

Let us return to Jacob Zuma and Schabir Shaik. We can now see that their appeal to the 'reciprocal altruism' that bound them is a curious amalgam of the sovereign, freely chosen, affective friendship celebrated by Montaigne and the less intimate relations in which friends, as a form of 'credit', are necessary to support you in an uncertain world and protect you from your enemies. (They are, in the strange etymology of the English word *economy* from the Greek *oikos* (home), the *domestic* relations that enable you to participate in the *general* economy.) Shaik and Zuma are right to claim that post-Apartheid South African law does not recognize such a concept of friendship as a legal relationship within public life. We can see from the fact that the Chief Justice fears Hal's retribution and that it lies within Henry's power to affirm his officer's action or punish him for it, that it is alive in the public world of Shakespeare's imagined worlds. The power of these plays lies in their capacity to affirm the necessity of the shift from 'honest friendship' to the dispassionate loneliness of the head that wears the crown, while simultaneously registering that move as a loss.

To whom do Zuma and Shaik correspond, in my somewhat whimsical comparison? At first sight, Zuma as heir apparent appears to be Hal, whereas Shaik, trying to become 'blessed' as his friend, is Falstaff. But Zuma is by far the more Falstaffian figure, the man who, once the laws of South Africa were at his commandment, as it were, adopted the old knight's pseudo-youthful lifestyle of untrammelled sexuality and charming roguishness. I pointed out above that Zuma did not have the opportunity to sign the Robben Island Shakespeare. He could have; he was there. But he wasn't one of the elite who could have shared their knowledge of Shakespeare in the single cells: he was a general prisoner, held in cells of up to 300 people – one of the initial illiterates who graduated from the Island a relatively educated man. His predecessor, Thabo Mbeki, was not on the Island; he spent his time abroad, graduating from Sussex University with a graduate degree in economics while his father, Govan, spent 27 years with Nelson Mandela in prison. As heir apparent, Thabo took over from Mandela as president of the country. Govan Mbeki marked Orsino's indulgently poetic disquisition on music as the food of love. What might his son have chosen, had he been there instead of in England?

Thabo Mbeki's choices are apparent in his fondness for quoting Shakespeare and other writers in his speeches while he was President. In the 2000 Oliver Thambo lecture, Mbeki began by recalling Shakespeare's *The Tempest*.[18] Tony Leon, the white leader of the opposition was likened to Prospero's evil brother, Antonio; Caliban was seen as the embodiment of the black petit bourgeoisie. By implication, Mbeki cast himself as the mage. This miniature reading of Shakespeare's play caused an uproar, especially among those who believed that they knew their Shakespeare. They declared that the president with intellectual pretensions most certainly did not. Did Mbeki not know what a howler he had committed? Everybody knows that Prospero is the evil white colonizer and Caliban the figure of the dispossessed and oppressed for whom those penned on a different island had suffered.[19] Billy Nair's choice of Caliban's charge, 'This island's mine . . .', shows that at least some of the Islanders would have read the play in this politically informed way.

But Mbeki turns out to be a pretty canny reader of Shakespeare. If Shakespeare gives the two Henrys almost identical speeches on the loneliness of kings – exemplified by what we could call their modern confinement to a world beyond friends – then Prospero exemplifies that loneliness. *The Tempest* is one of Shakespeare's most friendless plays: its two pairs of friends, Antonio and Sebastian and Stephano and Trinculo, are travesties or parodies of friendship. But Prospero is also a parody of the concept of kingship that Hal sought to achieve as Henry V. We may find Prospero bad-tempered, inconsistent, autocratic, aloof, even a liar; but there is one thing one can say of him: there are few people with whom he appears to have been capable of having a 'generally corrupt relationship'.

'I play the man I am'

Mbeki's solitariness is underscored by Mark Gevisser's recent biographical study, *The Dream Deferred*, which concludes by returning to the author's refrain about the former president's self-declared affinity with the tragic figure of Shakespeare's Coriolanus: Mbeki 'will not succumb to the injunctions of a family that has so brutally cast him out. He will attempt to avoid Coriolanus's fate by living with neither the Romans of his blood or the Volscians of his convictions . . . I conclude the book knowing that he is truly alone'.[20] In his biographer's eyes, Govan Mbeki's son would have gravitated towards *Coriolanus* had he been on Robben Island with his father, initiating and perpetuating what Gevisser considers to be a fundamental, perhaps even tragic, misreading of Shakespeare's play and character. Mbeki had 'discovered' *Coriolanus*, Gevisser tells us, in the early sixties (just when Mandela and his comrades were being tried) while he was at the Lenin Institute in Moscow. In his 'particularly eccentric reading', Mbeki had written to a friend extolling the Roman general's 'contempt "for the rabble, the unthinking mob"' (Gevisser, Kindle loc. 2792), as the heroic attribute of a true revolutionary; in Gevisser's judgement, Mbeki would have seen himself reflected in Coriolanus's rigid sense of his own untouchable integrity – 'Would you have me false to my nature? . . . I play the man I am' (*Coriolanus*, 3.2.14–16). Mbeki's behaviour at the momentous Polokwane conference, when he was ousted from his position as leader of the ANC by Jacob Zuma's supporters, reflected his Shakespearean hero's banishment of the mob and declaration of his own world 'elsewhere' (*Coriolanus*, 3.3.120–35). Prospero, Coriolanus, Mbeki. Who is to say that Mbeki's readings of Shakespeare were 'eccentric'? If anything, they were wholly focused on the person at the centre of the text: the person reading them.

Mbeki's responses to Shakespeare's pair of complex, indeed unfathomable, characters involved seeing them as mirrors of himself, unconcerned by the nuances of context and interpretative correctness. It is virtually unthinkable for Mandela or his comrades to have chosen either Prospero or Coriolanus as exemplars of themselves or their condition, because solitariness and exile – equally attributes of Mbeki, Prospero and Coriolanus – were the very opposite of the lived experience of the Robben Islanders. The Mbeki that Gevisser represents at the end of his biography – isolated by choice; bitter, aloof, refusing the political family of which he had been a part his whole life as much as they had rejected him – had moved from external exile into a form of internal banishment: cut off from comrades, countrymen and friends.

'Twin brothers'

I want to conclude at some distance from Robben Island and its copy of Shakespeare, on the topic of exile, friendship and betrayal, by returning to Hugh Lewin's experiences of his trial and imprisonment as a political prisoner in Pretoria. After I had been teaching his exemplary memoir of his trial and imprisonment, *Bandiet: Seven Years in a South African Prison*, as part of my prison-writing course at the University of Cape Town, I was fortunate enough to meet Lewin. He told me that there were things that he was unable to include in the book, and that he intended at some point to fill them in. The result, I thought at the time, was a new edition of the memoir, *Bandiet: Out of Jail*, published in 2002, essentially a reprint of the original, with some interesting addenda in the form of poetry, brief essays and stories and a harrowing account of fellow-prisoner Bram Fisher's horrendous medical maltreatment and death from cancer.[21] But in 2011 Lewin published a remarkable book called *Stones against the Mirror*.[22] I encountered it on a return to Cape Town when I had completed the first two chapters of this book. I was riveted. Here was the unfinished business Lewin had talked about.

Stones against the Mirror is a book about haunting: not by the ghost of a dead father but rather by the spectres of friends, two living and one dead. The dead friend is John Harris, a member of Lewin's group, the African Resistance Movement (ARM). Harris was the only white activist executed for political activities. He planted a bomb in the Johannesburg railway station after Lewin and others had been arrested, killing one person and injuring a number of others. Lewin's friends, Adrian Leftwich and John Lloyd, both gave testimony against Harris and his other comrades as state witnesses, and were permitted to leave the country for the United Kingdom, where both settled. One person against whom they gave witness was hanged and the others served long terms of imprisonment.

Prisoners on Robben Island write of being betrayed by comrades they thought of as their friends. Mandela, for example, writes:

> I was bewildered by Mtolo's betrayal. I never ruled out the possibility of even senior members breaking down under police torture. But by all accounts, Mtolo was never touched. On the stand, he went out of his way to implicate people who were not even mentioned in the case. It is possible, I know, to have a change of heart, but to betray so many others, many of whom were quite innocent, seemed to me inexcusable. (Kindle loc. 6642)

The possible explanation for his treachery is, however, suggested obliquely: 'During cross-examination we learned that Mtolo had been a petty criminal before joining MK and had been imprisoned three previous times for theft.'

Lewin does not have the comfort of inherent criminality to explain his betrayal by the man whom he considered his closest friend: his 'twin brother'. What he attempts to confront in the new book is a sense of complicity and intimacy that is as absent from Mandela's staunch solidarity as it is from Mbeki's solitary righteousness. Mandela can chart his memoirs as an inevitable and direct if delayed progress towards liberation – *Long Walk to Freedom*. Lewin's ironic acceptance of his caste as prisoner in the language of the jailer in his first book – *Bandiet* – is transformed into a shifting struggle for an identity in the second – *Stones against the Mirror*:

> Throw a clatter of memories at the mirror of your life and watch as the pieces scatter to the ground. There's no pattern. They glint in the shadows, demanding inspection, as you hesitate to choose which ones you'll pick up first. Some pieces choose themselves, however much you try to avoid them. (Lewin, *Stones*, 17)

If the South African polity that now exists in the aftermath of Mandela's struggle, Mbeki's technocratic rule and Zuma's shambolic negotiations among intestine factions, returns us to the Shakespearean concept of the 'friend' as he who has 'credit' and can support you, and if the notion of friendship on Robben Island is displaced or subsumed under the broader necessities of comradeship, Lewin's ghosts return us to earlier, classical notions of amity that are more single-mindedly exemplified by Aristotle and Montaigne: of the friend as the 'twin brother', the 'soul in two bodies'. In his plays Shakespeare offers at best imperfect representations of the Aristotelian ideal: in the erotic rivalry and reconciliation of Proteus and Valentine in *The Two Gentlemen of Verona*; in the politically compromised countenancing and subsequent banishment of Falstaff by Hal; in the feudal rivalry of the friends in *Two Noble Kinsmen*; in the somewhat distant admiration of Hamlet for Horatio; in the brutal betrayal of Banquo by Macbeth; and, perhaps most apposite in this context, in the troubled friendship of Cassius and Brutus in *Julius Casear*, both of whom are ultimately destroyed by a political purpose mobilized through the appeal of friendship.

I indicated in Chapter 1 that Brutus and Cassius do figure in the Robben Island Shakespeare, in Theo Chiba's choice of Brutus's pithy expression of the necessity of properly timed action – 'There is a tide in the affairs of men / Which, taken at the flood, leads on to fortune' (4.3.243–4). In its broader context, the speech registers the emotional ebb and flow of tension and empathy between friends, especially against a background of political choice and action. The friends, Brutus and Cassius, accuse each other of scanting their friendship through actions that involve both the sense of friendly 'credit' that I have been discussing and the broader political ideals of the revolution. Brutus has betrayed his friend Caesar in the most radical way for the sake of a political cause; now, seeking to defend their new order from Caesar's friend and nephew, Cassius and Brutus bitterly accuse each other of betrayal. Cassius charges his friend with ignoring his pleas to accommodate a comrade accused of accepting bribes. Brutus's intransigence is interpreted as a slight to the friendship itself, a rejection of the interceding friend who pleads for some expedient countenancing, and he responds with a call to remember what the Ides of March mean: commitment to a new order of justice that, by implication, should replace the 'credit' of countenancing friends:

Remember March, the ides of March remember;
Did not great Julius bleed for justice' sake?
What villain touched his body that did stab
And not for justice? What, shall one of us
That struck the foremost man of all this world
But for supporting robbers, shall we now

> Contaminate our fingers with base bribes,
> And sell the mighty space of our large honors
> For so much trash as may be grasped thus?
> I had rather be a dog and bay the moon
> Than such a Roman. (18–28)

There is a similar quarrel between Antony and Octavius in *Antony and Cleopatra*, but Shakespeare carefully evacuates it of all affective intimacy – Antony and Octavius are at best temporary allies, whereas Brutus and Cassius are friends, and the scene from *Julius Caesar* puts pressure on the complex interplay of the affective bonds of amity in the face of a world that works through reciprocal dealing in friendship as credit. The aggressive intensity of their anger is the necessary counterpart of their love for each other, and when their disagreement collapses under the sudden news of Portia's death, Cassius is all too ready to excuse Brutus's behaviour with heart-broken and self-recriminating empathy. That he is being manipulated by his friend totally and mistakenly secure in his own self-righteous opinion of himself does not detract from the scene's success as a depiction of the complexity of a particular concept of friendship in its need to negotiate a relentlessly political world alongside more intimate claims. There are so few depictions of this kind of friendship and its affective tensions in Robben Island memoirs because, whatever the centrality of politics to the Islanders, it was ultimately a politics at a remove from the demands of the world elsewhere.

There is one other area in which the constancy of friendship arises in the choice of Mandela's companions: the sonnets. Two sonnets that celebrate the constancy of loving friendship – 25 and 30 – were claimed by J. Nzuza and Don Davies, respectively, while Sonnet 123's defiance of time and its transformations in the context of close relationships appealed to Theo Cholo. The faithfulness claimed by the latter might have spoken to Cholo of a relationship of love, friendship or his commitment to the political struggle. In general terms, Shakespeare's sonnets are attempts to forge a personal space for friendship or love in a world where the separation of private and public spheres was in fact impossible. Mandela's regret that his political commitments had made him unavailable for an ordinary family life reflect a world in which the separation is already taken for granted, and where the imposition from the outside of politics is to be regretted alongside the recognition of its necessity. The very medium in which Shakespeare sought to proclaim his independence from 'public honour and proud titles' (sonnet 25) and his 'dear time's waste' (sonnet 30), by celebrating the mere thought of the friend, was irreducibly public.

The haunting of Lewin's life story by those of his friends attests to a very different attempt to negotiate private and public worlds. Unlike the Robben Islanders who record their time on the Island as a final victory over it – as a transcendence through which it was sublated in a Hegelian sense, overcome and also incorporated into their own progressive story of subjection, control and resurrection – Lewin admits that he continues to be 'haunted' by the prison. Like a modern-day Hamlet who can neither rid himself of the ghost of his father nor find a way of exorcizing that spectre by fulfilling its commandments, Lewin is finally twinned, through the prison, with the inverse image of Horatio: the friend unable to rise above the vicissitudes of fortune, who instead of offering to turn to the 'felicity' of suicide or even tell the still unknowing world of his friend's sacrifice, sacrifices his friend, like feeble Rosencrantz and Guildenstern, to the vultures of the state. In an incisive description of the position of his best friend – his twin brother – Lewin writes on hearing that Leftwich had been detained by the security police 'Jesus, I thought. *Adrian.* It's almost like they've got *me*' (*Stones*, 88). But during his testimony of his betrayal in *Bandiet*, and in a subsequently published poem, he observes: 'I sat in the dock where there was plenty of room, lots more room in the dock for others with us four accused. They stood alone, in the box, where there was room for one, like a coffin.'[23]

Lewin is too careful a writer to have overlooked the paradox of his pronominal use, in which the spatial relations that speak of isolation are contradicted by his grammar, which paradoxically couples *I* and *us* and *they* and *alone*: I *sat in the dock where there was plenty of room with* us *for* others . . . They *stood alone*. . . . The chiasmus of Lewin's initial description points forward to his haunting in *Stones against a Mirror* by the very ghosts that he had confined (or who had confined themselves) to the coffin of the witness box. By betraying the people whom he was supposed to have led and taken care of, Lewin's friend Adrian Leftwich had become *dead to him*:

> I used to believe that that they had put themselves inside a different kind of jail: a jail that had no keys. We served our sentences and were released, I used to say. They bought their freedom with pieces of silver and they would live with that knowledge for the rest of their days.
>
> It feels less simple, now. (*Stones*, 48)

Lewin's revisiting of the 'now' of that past certainty puts the notion of the present moment under pressure. The person represented as writing and thinking in this passage, so secure in his differentiated uses of the pronouns 'I', 'we' and 'they' – upon these foundation stones rested the whole edifice of Apartheid – is *now* no longer so secure that he knows the difference between the pronouns and their hoops of inclusion and exclusion.

Stones in a Mirror is the story of a man who no longer knows what he sees when he looks into the mirror of the present or the glass of his memory. It is the story of betrayal, but also of recovery, as Lewin discovers a path back to the friend who betrayed him. That path runs through the prison, not in despite of it. What Lewin discovers is not merely that the *I* is constituted through others – we should by now recognize this as a platitude – but also that the ethical security offered by a relatively stable communality – *we* – is always endangered and invaded by any excluded community, even the *they* who – necessarily singly – occupied the coffin of the witness box.

Lewin writes of his time as a white activist, 'it was a cascading, seductive time of intense relationships. You could never be close to someone who didn't hate the system. You chose your friends because they shared your ideals and your outrage. You had to trust each other absolutely . . .' (*Stones*, 46). When he needs to convey the greatest intensity of intimate relationships he has to make do with the distancing pronoun 'you', especially in its insidious relation to 'each other'. This is the language of community on Robben Island – the sense that friendship is comradeship: a shared set of ideals and values that necessarily bind through trust. Perhaps its greatest folly is the belief that friends are chosen, and that they are chosen for publicly available reasons like ideals, outrage or hatred of a system. For Lewin comes to discover that just as he did not choose his friendship with Adrian, betrayal could not be allocated along established pronominal lines.

In 1978 and 1979, at about the time when Mandela and his comrades were signing the Robben Island Shakespeare and the generation of white activists that followed Lewin were in Pretoria Local Prison, I was living scarcely a hundred yards away: in the officer's quarters of the South African Army Headquarters, in Potgieter Street. Having postponed my draft for national service for almost a decade as a student, I could stave off the inevitable fate no longer. I convinced myself that with an English graduate degree, as a language officer tasked with translations, editing, and once, writing a speech for the Minister of Defence, P. W. Botha – which briefly caught the attention of the Sunday papers for its unusually liberal tone – I could remain uncontaminated by the war that the South African government was fighting in Namibia, Angola and against its own people. For two years, in 1978 and 1979, I had an unimpeded view of Pretoria Local Prison across a barbed-wire fence from my room.

After completion of my service I went to the University of York, in England, where Lewin's friend, Leftwitch, had for almost 20 years held an academic post in the Department of Politics. I did not meet him. After an intense personal struggle recorded in *Stones against the Mirror*, Lewin did go to meet him, some 40 years after Leftwich had committed himself to the coffin of the witness box. It is not clear exactly what prompted Lewin to make this momentous journey back to his friend. Partly, his experience as a commissioner of the South African Truth and Reconciliation Commission and his subsequent investigations of atrocities in Cambodia and Burma pressed upon him the emptiness of retribution and revenge. Partly, Lewin comes to realize, with Montaigne, that friends are not chosen. While common experiences, background, values and outrage may play a role in the formation of friendships, they are not their cause. But mostly, I suspect, Lewin records a gradual sense of the permeability of the boundaries so deceptively held in place by the grammar of exclusion: between *us* and *them*, friend and enemy.

There are two betrayals in Lewin's account: Leftwich's betrayal of his best friend, and John Lloyd's betrayal of John Harris, their mutual friend, who had planted the bomb in Johannesburg railway station and was subsequently hanged as a result of that betrayal. Lloyd had not only given incriminating evidence against Harris, but after he had left for England he had refused to testify in mitigation of the death sentence. Harris haunts Lewin's book with particular intensity. He offers Lewin a moving, powerful occasion not only to excoriate the death penalty in general, but also to mourn the structural impossibility for mourning that its execution in South Africa imposed upon this heartless ritual of death.

In a haunting echo of Hamlet, Lewin observes that Harris asked, the day before he died, in a curiously detached formulation: 'What do they do with the body?' The executed prisoner's body is the property of the state, to dispose of as it sees fit. John Harris was cremated, and his ashes were kept for some years in the prison commandant's cupboard, until, as Lewin writes, 'they were rescued . . . by a prison chaplain, for secret burial in the condemned's corner of a Pretoria cemetery, under a gravestone that recorded only John's name and dates' (*Stones*, 120). Recently, a number of ANC political prisoners was reinterred with proper honours in Cape Town, reclaimed from the impersonal monster of the Apartheid state. We are once again haunted by *Hamlet*, not only in the almost exact question regarding Polonius's body, but also by the play's general concern with the impossibility of mourning the dead, of establishing proper relationships of ritual and memorial: from old Hamlet's murder to the alienation from family remembrance and ritual of Polonius and Ophelia, and, finally, in Hamlet's urgent request that his story be memorialized by his friend for the 'yet unknowing world'.

Lewin recounts an encounter with his police interrogator at a Truth Commission hearing that severely complicates the mirrors of memory and identity which sustain the senses of friendship and personal identity in the story of struggle, endurance and justification. Throughout his book he tells us that John Lloyd was the man who had betrayed John Harris – Lloyd was the friend who, under torture, gave Harris's name to the police. In both of his books Lewin tells of being beaten repeatedly, and then suddenly, of Lieutenant John Viktor coming in and saying triumphantly, '*Ons het hom*!' – 'We've got him!' – Harris.

Meeting Viktor again years later, Lewin records the inevitable sense of vulnerability of the tortured in the presence of the torturer, despite the formal turning of the tables:

> Viktor turned around, stretched out his hand and said: "So! It's Hugh, isn't it? Hugh Lewin." I took his outstretched hand.
>
> We both squeezed hard and stared at each other – and I said: "Yes, meneer Viktor, Hugh Lewin."
>
> And he smiled. "Hello Hughie." We dropped hands and stood facing each other . . . "yes," said Viktor. "Eight years . . . or was it seven? Seven years, wasn't it?"
>
> "Seven years. No remission."
>
> "Ja. I remember," he said, in control.

> I felt I was standing again inside that chalk circle on the floor in the interrogation room at the Grays, but I wasn't moving. "Yes," I said, "and Eisenstein and Hirson and Prager."
>
> "Ja," he said and turned to his lawyer. "There was this case and I tell you we gave these guys a bad time."
>
> You did, but I'm here now and I'm not moving. It was chummy, the three of us on the stage together, chatting amiably.
>
> "Funny," I said, "you look just like Dave Kitson, with your moustache and grey hair."
>
> . . .
>
> "Yes," said Viktor, "I remember: Ian David Kitson." Thirty-four years ago – before Soweto, Vlakplaas, Bisho, before all those events and all that time, Viktor remembered precisely: "Ian David Kitson."
>
> Then he floored me. "You gave us John Harris. Frederick John Harris." It was almost as if he was thanking me.
>
> But no. "But no," I said, "you had his name already." On that awful night at Grays, it was Viktor who had stopped Van der Merwe beating me when the floor above us had started to rumble. It was Viktor who had said, "Ons het hom," indicating upwards with his eyebrows.
>
> "No, I said, you've got it wrong. You had him already."
>
> He nodded, as if in recognition, but he wasn't really interested, he wasn't really listening . . . (*Stones*, 168–9)

It is a masterful recollection, of searing honesty. For at this point, in his encounter with his former interrogator, when Lewin should have been secure both politically and personally, the sense of moral integrity that has sustained him throughout his imprisonment and his subsequent life, collapses. We do not finally know whether Lewin's memory of what had actually happened – of who had betrayed the friend to the death – is accurate or not. Characteristically, Viktor doesn't care.

What matters is that Lewin's confidence is shaken by the encounter with the ghost of his past. Is the ghost a true messenger or is he Satan's envoy? Suddenly unsure, insecure in his distinctions between betrayer and betrayed, memory and falsehood, self and other, Lewin recognizes himself in the mirror of others.

> "The testimonies of the women," he writes, they dominate my memory of those years. Staunch and proud, they told their stories, talking not of themselves, but of their husbands and sons and fathers. The women who had borne the brunt of oppression and who now came to tell of the pain of others. They made only one demand: that the bones of their loved ones should be brought home.
>
> "Bring back the bones so that we know where they are."
>
> What about revenge and compensation or justice?
>
> "There's no point in seeking revenge. I forgive them because not doing so will not help me in any way."
>
> What can the commission do for you? We asked the witnesses. Nothing, they replied, just bring us back their bones – and let them tell us why it happened. If we know why, then we can understand. It is not a question of forgiveness; it is a question of knowing. (*Stones*, 177)

Lewin represents the voices of the women who testified before the TRC as a single chorus identified by quotation marks: *their* voices, from which he has learned to reconsider his own position. And as his account drops the quotation marks, he subsumes their voices into his own: 'Nothing, they replied . . .' Or was it '"Nothing", they replied . . .'? Or, perhaps, 'Nothing, I replied . . .'? That is not to say that Lewin's and the voices of the women are either completely separate or identical. He has undoubtedly learned from them. His own return to the bones of his friendship with Adrian Leftwich is also both a question of knowing and forgiveness. But perhaps it is neither.

At the end of his book Lewin records his correspondence with another friend, Jock Strachan, who had spent time with him in prison, and who advises him: 'You don't have anything other than your own recollections . . . why not make technique and style as important as content? The risk otherwise is of falling into archival truth' (187). 'Well, dear reader,' Lewin writes, 'treat it as fiction. That's what I'd advise' (187). Where can one commit one's memories? To whom dare one entrust one's dreams?

Coda

Robben Island is currently a museum: a place of remembrance for the prisoners who suffered there and their courageous struggle against the cruelty of racism and authoritarianism. The Island is thus a monument and a memorial. It is held up not only as testimony to a set of events, but also as witness to the making of a new country and a transformed set of values and ideals. It is Cape Town's most popular tourist destination. Its material palpability – its rocks, sand, sea, the quarries, stone houses, roads, crumbling gravestones, the solidity of the prison itself, even the vast dome of the sky above it – speaks of its indubitable reality, of the quiddity of history and truth. And yet its rocks, stone and gates of steel do not speak of their own accord: they require the equivalent of Shakespeare's 'powerful rhyme' and 'black lines' to maintain the 'living record of its memory' (sonnet 55).

Like 55, sonnet 65 is frequently anthologized for its universal meditation on the corrosive effects of time and the problem of countering or evading the mortality that is the very condition of the world. It is one of the sonnets chosen by Neville Alexander, author of *A Robben Island Dossier*. The other is sonnet 60:

Since brass, nor stone, nor earth, nor boundless sea,
But sad mortality o'ersways their power,
How with this rage shall beauty hold a plea,
Whose action is no stronger than a flower?
O, how shall summer's honey breath hold out
Against the wreckful siege of batt'ring days,
When rocks impregnable are not so stout,
Nor gates of steel so strong, but Time decays?
O fearful meditation! Where, alack,
Shall Time's best jewel from Time's chest lie hid?
Or what strong hand can hold his swift foot back?
Or who his spoil of beauty can forbid?
O, none, unless this miracle have might,
That in black ink my love may still shine bright.

It would be presumptuous to guess at Alexander's personal reasons for choosing this sonnet. It holds two things in tension: on the one hand, it reflects on the inevitability of time's destruction of human constructions and the material things of nature (which might be a consoling thought to someone confined by 'rocks impregnable' and 'gates of steel'); on the other, it confronts the decaying force of time that not only affects brass, stone, earth and sea, but also destroys memory, obliterating history, both of which have as a result to be preserved in 'black ink'.

Theo Cholo chose sonnet 123, which begins as a defiant challenge to the transformative effects of time that Shakespeare laments in sonnets 55, 60 and 65 – 'No, Time, thou shalt not boast that I do change' – and ends with an absolute affirmation of truth and constancy: 'This I do vow, and this will ever be: / I will be true, despite thy scythe and thee.' Such determination would have struck a chord with many on the Island, whose experiences of time included the incorrigible slowness of its passing rather than its 'continual haste'. At the same time, the defiant determination not to succumb to change betrays the very possibility of personal change and loss of memory, of the repression with which I began and that is Cooper's abiding concern.

Cholo's choice of a poem that celebrates absolute truth and total constancy across time is peculiarly ironic but also apposite in the light of systematic attempts to preserve the memory encapsulated by Robben Island. For, invited to comment on his choice in 2008, Cholo remarked that he would now choose a different sonnet; that 'he didn't like it nearly as much as he liked Sonnet 122'.[24] That sonnet is if anything even more concerned with the preservation and loss of memory; but instead of the lofty certainty of sonnet 65 or the strained protestation of 123, 122 negotiates a more personal accusation of betrayal and forgetfulness:

> Thy gift, thy tables, are within my brain
> Full character'd with lasting memory,
> Which shall above that idle rank remain
> Beyond all date, even to eternity;
> Or at the least, so long as brain and heart
> Have faculty by nature to subsist;
> Till each to raz'd oblivion yield his part
> Of thee, thy record never can be miss'd.
> That poor retention could not so much hold,
> Nor need I tallies thy dear love to score;
> Therefore to give them from me was I bold,
> To trust those tables that receive thee more.
> To keep an adjunct to remember thee
> Were to import forgetfulness in me.

It's a complex poem; it echoes Hamlet's urgent declaration, in response to the ghost's injunction to remember him:

> Remember thee!
> Ay, thou poor ghost, whiles memory holds a seat
> In this distracted globe. Remember thee!

> Yea, from the table of my memory
> I'll wipe away all trivial fond records,
> All saws of books, all forms, all pressures past,
> That youth and observation copied there;
> And thy commandment all alone shall live
> Within the book and volume of my brain,
> Unmix'd with baser matter. (1.5.95–104)

The point is that in both cases the preservation of memory is an ethical injunction and an accepted responsibility. In sonnet 122 what seems to be an act of betrayal in the poet's giving away of a gift (these 'tables' are a book which, as a gift, is both a record of the relationship and something in which to remember it by writing in it),[25] is in fact the strongest sign of his complete commitment, since he declares that his memory lies not in some inanimate object but rather in what he has experienced, thought and felt in the immediacy of his relationship: 'Thy gift, thy tables, are within my brain / Full character'd with lasting memory.' Hamlet is less assured than the poet of the sonnets; he is aware of the tendency of other thoughts, experiences and feelings to displace or disrupt the complete retention of loyal memory. Hence his determination to displace *everything else* with the memory of his father. But Hamlet forgets: the play shows that the notion of memory as a mere record is unsustainable and unlivable.

Venkatrathnam's Shakespeare is a 'book and volume' as Hamlet puts it, of memory and forgetfulness in equal measure.

In December 2011 I visited the Island as a part of a tourist group to remind myself of that quiddity, and to revisit places and experiences from my earlier pilgrimages. I knew from my previous tours that the promise that, because you would be taken through the prison by an ex-prisoner you would gain access to an authentic experience, could not be taken at face value. You would know this only from multiple visits. Each guide tells a different story, depending on his time and place of imprisonment, his political affiliation and personal responses. On this trip in particular I wished to revisit the leper cemetery – especially the coupled graves of the Fermers who had died, after being separated across a hundred yards, within an hour of each other – which I recalled from the occasion on which I had been able to spend a weekend on the island as part of a retreat held by my wife's Law Race and Gender Centre at the University of Cape Town. The cemetery had haunted me for some years, and I wanted to get a picture of especially the Fermers' grave, which I remembered only dimly, having forgotten their names and its exact location in the thorn-strewn graveyard. I did not know how I would take my photograph, since the cemetery was not part of the strictly controlled tour. I hoped that I would be able to slip away, somehow, find it among the thousand others, and slip back to the official tour.

It was only when I was watching the film shown on the pixilated television screens on the modernized ferry (which I had not seen on earlier visits) that I was struck by the ways in which the museum was engaged as much in the erasure of memory as its preservation. Against the voice recounting the usual Robben Island story, an even more grainy film appeared of a group of officials and civilians being taken on a tour of the prison. The tour had been arranged for foreign and local journalists in 1977, although the commentary did not say this. There were Mandela, Sisulu and company in their cells – but the cells were very different from the standard picture that the world now knows so well, from the internet, books and their careful preservation on the Island itself: of the bare concrete floor, the small wooden bench and the folded grey blanket seen through the barred gate – the epitome of comfortless bleakness and deprivation. The cell in the film that flickered above me and the heads of some 500 other tourists contained beds, pillows, blankets, a table and chair, bookcases with books, a number of green tomatoes, the famous *National Geographic* picture of the naked woman running on the beach and a photograph of Mandela's wife, Winnie. Where did those come from? I thought. Had they been put in deliberately as a propaganda exercise for the international press? That would not have been the first time such things had happened. But what we saw, briefly, on the TV monitors on the ferry, and which contradicted so starkly what we were about to see on the Island, was a set of cells approximately as they were in 1977, the year in which most of Mandela's comrades signed Venkatrathnam's Shakespeare.

A Prisoner in the Garden, a book collection of photos, letters and notes from Mandela's time in prison, contains four photographs of his cell that resemble the TV pictures. In a lengthy caption, the dates on which they might have been taken are the subject of an earnest deliberation by Ahmed Kathrada and Mac Maharaj, who determine from the layout and the furniture that they had been variously taken between 1971 and 1977.[26] The cell presented as 'Mandela's cell' to the tourist on Robben Island is a moment deliberately frozen in time and represented as the unchanging condition of 27 years. It is a memorial inscription that, in being set down, obliterates all other 'trivial fond records'. The cells along the corridor of B section containing Mandela's are currently empty. It might have been a intriguing exercise in the preservation of memory, I thought, as I stood in line to pay homage to the presented cell, to be offered a variety of differently furnished cells, to convey the fact that time moved even on Robben Island – that things changed, and that such change is testimony of the agency of the prisoners in shaping even this restricting world.

On the tour I discovered that there is indeed an attempt to do that with the solitary house in which Robert Sobukwe, president of the PAC, was kept, in isolation, for 6 years, 'at the pleasure of the state'. Both the house and Sobukwe's memory are marginal to the central story the museum currently tells. Unlike the other political prisoners, Sobukwe was not confined on Robben Island by any guilty verdict and sentence in a court of law. He was confined in a small dwelling by a special act of parliament, and not allowed any contact with the other prisoners.

Sobukwe's presence has, like the operation of Hamlet's tables, been all but erased by the preservation of Mandela's memory. The bus that takes one on an initial tour of the island stops briefly outside the house, and a short account is given of his incarceration, before you move on for a 20-minute refreshment break in the village. During this break my companion, a historian specializing in South African museums, recognized our guide as one of his former students. When asked why we had not gone into Sobukwe's house, the guide explained that it took too long and was too much trouble, but that if we were willing to curtail our tour of the central prison he would give us a private tour of the Sobukwe house. Happily, the walk took us past the leper cemetery, which I was able to visit once again.

The exhibition in/of the house is small but striking. The Robben Island Museum has reconstructed his bedroom-office, complete with table, chair, bedstead and 1960s' mustard-yellow radio; there are letters to and from his wife on the walls; and in an adjoining room, a life-sized photograph of Sobukwe in crisp trousers and white shirt (since he was not officially a prisoner) ironing his civilian clothes. In another room are four large prison bedsteads where his children slept when, for 2 weeks in January 1978, his family was permitted to stay with him. In the same room, displayed in a large glass case in the centre, like the Shakespeare that I saw in Nash House in Stratford, is a large, open book. It is the prison register where, in red ink, Robert Sobukwe's arrival is recorded with the comment 'At the pleasure of the state,' Prospero's books, I thought. But which one – the Shakespeare or the ledger of vindictive incarceration?

In 2012 the 'book and volume' of Robben Island is contested, subject to political and ideological struggles in which the meaning of South Africa's history and future are staked. I have mentioned the ways in which the record of the Apartheid prison has itself obliterated aspects of history and suffering, from the lepers and outcasts of previous centuries, through the experience of women political prisoners, to the failure of many prisoners to recognize themselves in the mirror of the Robben Island Shakespeare. This peculiar Shakespeare text is part of the memory through which its former inhabitants will live on 'in the eyes of posterity'; but giving them such life is not a simple matter. I have ventured to discern the people and the experiences within those signatures. But such a venture is fraught with difficulties, uncertainties and dangers. At most I have conjured a few shadows from this historical conjunction of Shakespeare's extraordinary text and the unique marks of the proper names inscribed in its pages. In doing so, the unconscious I have been trying to discern along the lines of the palimpsest of these tables has, I fear, largely been my own.

Notes

Introduction

1. The Episcopalian Church in the United States of America.
2. This is true. The headmaster saw me laughing in this way and gave me six strokes for supposedly telling jokes in chapel.
3. There is a story that underscores the uncanny probability of Shakespearean coincidence and that happened some 40 years later, at the World Shakespeare Congress in Brisbane, Australia, in 2005. Seeing me wandering on my own at the opening reception a friend jokingly offered to introduce me to somebody. The first passing woman he grabbed at random turned out to be Monica, the daughter of the woman who had played the Marlowe Society Shakespeare records for me. Monica was the first girl I kissed.
4. In 1973, the Assembly decided, on the recommendation of the Special Committee, that the South African regime had no right to represent the people of South Africa, and that the liberation movements recognized by the OAU were 'the authentic representatives of the overwhelming majority of the South African people'. It requested all intergovernmental organizations to deny membership to the South African regime and to invite the liberation movements to participate in their meetings. (Enuga S. Reddy, 'United Nations and the International Campaign against Apartheid' (scnc.ukzn.ac.za/doc/AAmwebsite/AAMCONFpapers/Reddy,ES.doc, accessed 11 September 2011). See also:

    30 November, International Convention on the Suppression and Punishment of the Crime of Apartheid approved by the General Assembly [Resolution 3068(XXVIII)].

    14 December, The General Assembly declared that the South African regime has 'no right to represent the people of South

Africa' and that the liberation movements recognized by the OAU are 'the authentic representatives of the overwhelming majority of the South African people' [Resolution 3151 G (XXVIII)] (www.sahistory.org.za/organisations/timeline-united-nations-and-apartheid-1946–1994).

5. When it was not vilified as 'Hell-hole', Robben Island was regarded the 'Isle of Purgatory': 'For prisoners on transportation, the island Prison was true Purgatory: a half way point between the Cape and the feared settlements of Van Dieman's Land or New South Wales' (Harriet Deacon, *Essential Robben Island* (Cape Town: David Philip Publishers, 1997)).
6. Martin Orkin, *Shakespeare against Apartheid* (Craighall, Johannesburg: Ad. Donker, 1987).
7. David Johnson, *Shakespeare and South Africa* (Oxford: Clarendon, 1996).
8. Natasha Distiller, *South Africa, Shakespeare, and Post-Colonial Culture* (New York: Edwin Mellen Press, 2005).
9. Lewis Nkosi, *Home and Exile* (London: Longmans, 1983), 13.
10. Nelson Mandela, *Long Walk to Freedom* (London: Holt, Rinehart and Winston, 2000), 450.
11. Merton Dagutt, quoted in Benjamin Pogrund, *Sobukwe and Apartheid* (New Brunswick, NJ: Rutgers Univerity Press, 1991), 63.
12. Anders Hallengren, 'Nelson Mandela and the rainbow of Culture', (www.nobelprize.org/nobel_prizes/peace/laureates/1993/mandela-article.html (acccssed 4 December 2011)). Also Anders Hallengren, *Nobel Laureates in Search of Identity & Integrity: Voices of Different Cultures* (Singapore: World Scientific, 2004).
13. Sampson, *Mandela,* 230. Of course, it is probably Hallengren echoing Sampson.
14. Tom Lodge, *Mandela: A Critical Life* (Oxford: Oxford University Press, 2006). No actual evidence is offered for this claim.
15. Isabel Hofmeyr, 'Reading Debating/Debating Reading: The Case of the Lovedale Literary Society, or Why Mandela Quotes Shakespeare', in *Africa's Hidden Histories: Everyday Literacy and Making the Self,*

African Expressive Cultures, ed. Karin Barber (Bloomington, IN: Indiana University Press, 2006), 258–77 (258).

16. One among some 160 objects on display, the Robben Island Shakespeare has been called a 'prize' and 'iconic' exhibit. See, for example, 'British Museum to display Robben Island copy of Shakespeare's works' (www.telegraph.co.uk/culture/9407821/British-Museum-to-display-Robben-Island-copy-of-Shakespeares-works.html; accessed 25 July 2012); 'Mandela and the Robben Island Bible' (http://thelastword.msnbc.msn.com/_news/2012/07/18/12819014-mandela-and-the-robben-island-bible?lite; (accessed 25 July 2012); 'Nelson Mandela's Shakespeare edition to go on display' (www.bbc.co.uk/news/entertainment-arts-18502371; accessed 25 July 2012) and John Carlin, 'To Kill or not to Kill' (www.ft.com/intl/cms/s/2/ca921646-caed-11e1–8872–00144feabdc0.html#axzz21f6NZrAJ; accessed 25 July 2012). It is unusual for the BBC to have have made such a fundamental mistake as to attribute the copy of Shakespeare to Mandela rather than Venkatrathnam, thereby allowing myth to overwhelm reality.
17. Kathrada, *Letters*, 38. This statement is made in the context of his concern over the well-being of Sylvia Neal (referred to in the letter as 'Khala'), and the definite article suggests a specific set of passages which he shares either with her or other outsiders who are party to the letter.
18. 'I filled seven notebooks of quotes . . . Shakespeare quotes could fill a book. My book (Complete Works), which has been with me in various prisons, is this one, is marked all over. You don't know where to start stop with Shakespeare. There is just too much' (Unpublished Hahn interview, 8 October 2008).
19. Quoted in Sahem Venter, *A Free Mind: Ahmed Kathrada's Notebook from Robben Island* (Johannesburg: Jacana, 2005), 43. I shall come back to this when I discuss prisoners' affirmation of Shakespeare's universality.
20. An article in the *Toronto Star* reports an ANC spokeman's repudiation of the importance of Shakespeare or the Robben Island text for the anti-Apartheid struggle:

The British Museum believes it has the perfect final act to its Shakespeare exhibit – the so-called Robben Island Bible, a copy of the legendary playwright's complete works that reportedly gave solace to Nelson Mandela and other apartheid-era political prisoners during their detention on the South African island.

But Mandela's party, the ANC, vehemently disputes the book's 'iconic' status. 'It's iconic to those who want to make it iconic. To us, it is not,' said Jackson Mthembu, the ANC's national spokesman. 'It was not an inspiration.'

Unlike the Freedom Charter, a document that outlined a vision for a democratic, multiracial government in South Africa, the 'Bible' didn't play a role in the struggle against Apartheid, he told the Star.

'We know so many other documents that are iconic in the ANC's eyes. We didn't know anything called the Robben Island Bible.'

For prisoners, the book was nothing more than a study aid, Mthembu said, adding that reading Shakespeare wasn't a communal activity.

'African National Congress disputes "iconic" status of Robben Island Bible displayed in British Museum' (www.thestar.com/news/world/article/1229077-african-national-congress-disputes-iconic-status-of-robben-island-bible-displayed-in-british-museum; accessed 25 July 2012).

21. It is difficult to categorize all the writings from Robben Island under the terms 'memoir' or 'autobiography', since some are collections of letters, some collations of memorable quotations, others explicitly 'factional', while others present essays and reflections of a political and sociological character. Dennis Brutus, *A Simple Lust: Collected Poems of South African Jail & Exile Including Letters to Martha* (London: Heinemann, 1973), D. M. Zwelonke, *Robben Island*, African Writers Series 128 (London: Heinemann, 1973), Moses Dlamini, *Robben Island, Hell-Hole: Reminiscences of a Political Prisoner in South Africa* (Trenton, NJ: Africa World Press, 1984), Indres Naidoo, *Island in Chains: Prisoner 885/63 Ten Years on Robben Island* (Harmondsworth: Penguin, 1982), N. Alexander, *Robben Island Dossier 1964–1974*

(Cape Town: University of Cape Town Press, 1998), Natoo Babenia and Iain Edwards, *Memoirs of a Saboteur: Reflections on My Political Activity in India and South Africa* (Bellville: Mayibuye Books, 1995), Nelson Mandela, *Long Walk to Freedom* (London: Holt, Rinehart and Winston, 2000), Eddie Daniels, *There and Back: Robben Island, 1964–1979*, Mayibuye History and Literature Series no. 83 (Bellville, South Africa: Mayibuye Books, 1998), Robben Island Memories Series No. 4 (Cape Town, South Africa: Zebra and the Robben Island Museum, 2001), Govan Mbeki, *Learning from Robben Island: The Prison Writings of Govan Mbeki* (London: J. Currey, 1991), Ahmed Kathrada, *No Bread for Mandela: Memoirs of Ahmed Kathrada, Prisoner No. 468/64*, Reprint (Lexington, KY: The University Press of Kentucky, 2010), Sahm Venter (ed.), *A Free Mind: Ahmed Kathrada's Notebook from Robben Island* (Johannesburg: Jacana, 2005), Sedick Isaacs, *Surviving in the Apartheid Prison: Robben Island: Flash Backs of an Earlier Life* (Bloomington, IN: Xlibris Corporation, 2010).

22. See Desai, pp. 26, 76 and 105.
23. There is no way of knowing this for certain, but one can deduce it from the dates on which prisoners signed the book. Mandela, for example, marks his passage from *Julius Caesar* the day after Toivo ja Toivo signed the book. Mandela may well have read all of *Julius Caesar* in a day, but it is unlikely.
24. Kathrada notes that during the peculiarly repressive regime of Colonel Badenhorst beginning in January 1971, all books that were not directly relevant to their studies, including Shakespeare, were confiscated (Venter, *A Free Mind*, 53).
25. http://robbenislandbible.blogspot.com/search?updated-max=2010–02–18T07%3A39%3A00Z&max-results=7 (accessed 22 August 2011).
26. 'African National Congress disputes "iconic" status of Robben Island Bible displayed in British Museum' (www.thestar.com/news/world/article/1229077-african-national-congress-disputes-iconic-status-of-robben-island-bible-displayed-in-british-museum; accessed 25 July 2012). The report is mistaken in at least one respect, since it is very unlikely that Kathrada does not remember Venkatrathnam.
27. Interview with Hahn, 8 February 2008.

28. Jacques Derrida, 'Siganture Event Context', in *Limited Inc* (Evanston, IL: Northwestern University Press, 1978).

Chapter 1

1. Harriet Deacon, *The Island: A History of Robben Island, 1488–1990* (Cape Town: David Philip, 1996), 6. Living conditions for all of these groups were harsh, but perhaps the most moving plight was that of the lepers. From the 1840s until 1931 all people diagnosed with leprosy were forcibly removed to the island, where, with no recourse to appeal or review, they were held until their death. The graveyard bears poignant testimony to these people who suffered under the arbitrary oppression of an utterly misguided medical establishment. Married couples were forcibly separated, never to see each other again, even though they lived within a couple of hundred metres of one another. In the sorely neglected leper graveyard two graves, side by side, bear an elderly couple – Frederich and Wilhelmina Ferner – who died within an hour of each other. The leper hospital is now displayed to tourists as the site of the primary school for warders' children when the Island was converted into a prison: all traces of its former use are obscured.
2. For a philosophical account of the word, see Jacques Derrida, 'Racism's last word', *Critical Inquiry*, 12 (Autumn 1985): 290–9.
3. Dlamini, *Robben Island, Hell-Hole*, 23. For an account of such stereotyping, see David Schalkwyk, 'The rules of physiognomy: reading the convict in South African prison', *Pretexts*, 7.1 (1998): 81–96.
4. In the Rivonia trial, named after the rural suburb of Johannesburg in which the ANC had its operational headquarters, which was raided by the police in 1963, virtually the whole command of the ANC was sentenced to lengthy prison terms on Robben Island. They included Nelson Mandela, Walter Sisulu, Govan Mbeki, Ahmed Kathrada, Elias Motsoaledi, Andrew Mhlangeni, Billy Nair, Wilton Mkwayi and Raymond Mhlaba. Over a decade later they were all signatories of the Robben Island Shakespeare.

5. Neville Alexander provides a dispassionate account of the changing conditions on Robben Island in *Robben Island Dossier 1964–1974* (Cape Town: University of Cape Town Press, 1998).
6. For a more complete history of the Island, see Deacon, *The Island*. For specific accounts of prisoner experiences after 1963, see the memoirs listed in note 19 in the Introduction above.
7. 'Restoring dignity for those who died during incarceration on Robben Island', www.robben-island.org.za/index.php?option=com_content&view=article&id=86:restoring-dignity-for-those-who-died-during-incarceration-on-robben-island&catid=3:news&Item (accessed 9 September 2011).
8. These stories are repeated in countless prisoner memoirs and biographies of Nelson Mandela.
9. Deacon, *The Island*, 181, fn. 26.
10. Fran Lisa Buntman, *Robben Island and Prisoner Resistance to Apartheid* (Cambridge: Cambridge University Press, 2003): 'these little movies and other things people have put out [are] actually a romanticised version [of Robben Island]. . . . What I am objecting to is this idyllic picture of [Robben Island as a] great university, [where there was a] sharing of experience. . . . When the sordidness of prison behaviour is examined there is little difference between common law and political prisoners generally. Where the former are often organised into deadly rival gangs, the latter are organised into often warring political groupings' (143).
11. See Desai, *Reading Revolution*, 12, for an image of the page.
12. Eddie Daniels in Hahn interview, 3 February 2010.
13. See Sampson, 285–9: 'Mbeki was always strongly opposed to a broad front against apartheid: race oppression, he insisted, was born of class conflict . . . he strongly contradicted Mandela . . . [Mandela] and Mbeki were barely on speaking terms, and sometimes Walter Sisulu had to act as peacemaker' (287–8).
14. Personal e-mail correspondence, 15 March 2012.
15. http://robbenislandbible.blogspot.com/2010/02/monday-8-february-2010.html (accessed 21 March 2012).

16. '"Corruption was the main complaint the party heard from voters", said Sandi Sijake, president of the ANC's Veterans' League. "The problem is with ourselves in the ANC,"' Sijake said. 'ANC anger over campaign shambles', *Mail and Guardian*, 25 April 2011 (http://mg.co.za/article/ 2011–04–21-anc-irate-about-campaign; accessed 14 September 2011).
17. Thanks to Gail Paster for this observation. It speaks of the early antagonism between the ANC and PAC that some PAC members were hoping that Mandela and his comrades at the Rivonia trial would be sentenced to death (Meredith, *Mandela*, 247–8).
18. Hofmeyr notes that the topic of the Lovedale debating society recorded in the minutes of 1 April 1939 is the question: 'Are the uses of adversity sweet?' (268).
19. *Mandela: The Authorized Portrait* (Kansas City, MO: Andrews McMeel Publishers, 2006), 169.
20. See www.sabctrc.saha.org.za/hearing.php?id=56411&t=gqirana&tab=hearings and www.sabctrc.saha.org.za/hearing.php?id=55323&t=gqirana&tab=hearings and www.robbenislandbible.blogspot.com/ (accessed 21 March 2012).
21. See also Naidoo, *Island in Chains*, 214–15.
22. *The Road to Democracy: South Africans Telling their Stories, Volume 1* (South African Democracy Education Trust), 347–8. Available at: www.sadet.co.za/docs/RTD/stories/Stories%20-%20Justice%20Mpanza.pdf (accessed 19 September 2011).
23. Natoo Babenia and Iain Edwards, *Natoo Babenia: Memoirs of a Saboteur* (Belville: Mayibuye Books, 1995).
24. There is something peculiarly horrible about this in the light of the notorious fact that Dirk Coetzee's counter-insurgency group at Vlakplaas would torture their victims to death and then burn the bodies on huge fires while themselves barbequing meat and drinking beer. For an account of the members of the death squads who tortured and murdered opponents of Apartheid in the eighties, see Jacques Pauw, *Into the Heart of Darkness: Confessions of Apartheid's Assassins* (Johannesburg: Jonathan Ball, 1997).

25. Elaine Scarry, *The Body in Pain: The Making and Unmaking of the World* (New York: Oxford University Press, 1987).
26. Virginia Woolf, 'On being ill', *Collected Essays*, Vol. 4 (New York: Harcourt, 1976), 194.
27. Although see Ludwig Wittgenstein's counterargument that pain marks the foundation of human commonality, in *Philosophical Investigations*, trans. G. E. M. Anscombe (Oxford: Blackwell, 1973).
28. See also Dingake, 96, passim.
29. Sedick Isaacs, *Surviving in the Apartheid Prison: Robben Island: Flash Backs of an Earlier Life* (Bloomington, IN: Xlibris Corporation, 2010).
30. He was also one of only four political prisoners subjected to punishment by flogging, strapped to a steel frame and whipped across his back. 'It was not the searing pain that seemed to come as an explosion that took my breath away and had the greater impact, but rather the thought that fellow human beings were doing this to me in a completely cold blooded manner . . . The Security Police with their electric generators, their rubber batons for damaging the internal organs . . . and their brutality were after information. Here the brutality was an end in itself' (Kindle loc. 2488).
31. Sol. T Plaatje, *The Boer War Diary of Sol T. Plaatje; an African at Mafeking* (Johannesburg: Macmillan, 1973).
32. Sol T. Plaatje, 'The mote and the beam: an epic on sex-relationship 'twixt White and Black in British South Africa', in *Sol Plaatje: Selected Writings* (Johannesburg: Witwatersrand University Press, 1997).
33. Daniel Jones and Sol T. Plaatje, *A Sechuana Reader* (Farnborough: Gregg, 1970).
34. Sol T. Plaatje, *Sechuana Proverbs with Literal Translations and their European Equivalents* (London: K. Paul, Trench, Trubner & Co, 1916).
35. Sol T. Plaatje, *Native Life in South Africa: Before and Since the European War and the Boer Rebellion* (Johannesburg: Ravan Press, 1982).
36. Israel Gollancz, *A Book of Homage to Shakespeare* (Oxford: University Press, 1916).
37. See William Cobbett, *Rural Rides* (Harmondsworth: Penguin, 2001).

38. Orkin, *Shakespeare against Apartheid*.
39. See Jacques Derrida, 'Living on/border lines', trans. James Hulbert, in *Deconstructionism and Criticism*, ed. Harold Bloom et al. (New York: Seabury Press, 1979), 75–176.
40. Frank Anthony, as far as I can ascertain, marked almost the whole of the opening scene.
41. Desai reminds us that Mandela recalled Cassius's words 'the fault, dear Brutus, is not in our stars / . . . But in ourselves that we are underlings' in the drawing up of the manifesto of the Youth League of the ANC in 1944. He also recalls the *Drum* generation's affinity with Shakespeare in statements by Can Themba, Blake Modisane and Lewis Nkosi. For an extended discussion of Shakespeare's role in the lives of those writers and South Africa more generally, see Natasha Distiller, *South Africa, Shakespeare, and Post-Colonial Culture*.
42. It is telling to note Mandela's subsequent observation on fear and courage: 'I learned that courage was not the absence of fear, but the triumph over it. I felt fear myself more times than I can remember, but I hid it behind a mask of boldness. The brave man is not he who does not feel afraid, but he who conquers that fear' (*Long Walk*, Kindle loc. 11188).
43. A universal perception of Mandela at this time and subsequent to his release is his remarkable self-control. For further discussion of this aspect of his character, see David Schalkwyk, 'Mandela's stoicism', in *The Cambrdge Companion to Mandela*, ed. Rita Barnard (Cambridge: Cambridge University Press, forthcoming).
44. Quatro was called after a notorious Apartheid prison, 'The Fort', in Johannesburg, now the site of the Constitutional Court. For an account of the Quatro controversy, see the Reports of the Commission of Enquiry into Certain Allegations of Human Rights Abuse against ANC Prisoners and Detainees by ANC Members (Motsuenyane Commission Report), 20 August 1993; the Report of the Commission of Enquiry into Complaints by Former African National Congress Prisoners and Detainees (Skweyiya Commission Report), 1992; and Stephen Ellis, 'Mbokondo: Security in ANC camps, 1960–1990', *African Affairs*, 93 (1994): 279–98. Also David

Schalkwyk, 'Mandela's lost manuscript: appropriation and repression in accounts of Robben Island', *Prison Writings*, ed. Danine Farquharson. Available at: www.interdisciplinarypress.net/index2.php?page=shop.product_details&product_id=190&flypage=flypage.tpl&pop=1&option=com_virtuemart&Itemid=28.

45. See Mandela, *Long Walk*: 'I wanted these young men to see that the ANC was a great tent that could accommodate many different views and affiliations' (Kindle loc. 8757).
46. Mandela was aware of the abuses at such camps in the early 1970s. In *Long Walk* he records having heard of the abuses and deciding to contact the head of the ANC in exile, Oliver Thambo, about them: 'Jimmy [April] regaled us with war stories, but I also took him aside and asked him about MK's problems. . . . He told me stories of discontent in the camps, and of abuses by MK officers, I asked him to keep the matter to himself, and I managed to smuggle a letter out to Oliver suggesting that some reforms must be made in the camps' (Kindle loc. 8340). The worst abuses occurred after 1976, when the ANC had to deal with the defiant youthful generation of the 'Soweto uprising'.
47. Strini Moodley, interviewed by John Carlin. Available at: www.pbs.org/wgbh/pages/frontline/shows/mandela/interviews/moodley.html (accessed 5 September 2002).
48. See www.ever-fasternews.com/index.php?php_action=read_article&article_id=343 (accessed 16 October 2011):

> The same logic led this champion of youthful revolt into the notorious 'Iran' prison run by the ANC in exile for its own dissenting members in Luanda in Angola, where he was tortured by members of his own organisation. Finding himself in exile in a top–down political organisation structured similarly to its major funder, the Soviet Union, Motapanyane's critical and democratic spirit nurtured on the events of '76 made him powerful enemies in the older generation of exile apparatchiks.
>
> For his misery in detention and in exile, Motapanyane blamed above all Andrew Masondo – political activist of the Fifties and Sixties generation, Robben Island veteran, one of the architects of the ANC's system of prison camps in exile for its own members,

principal of the Solomon Mahlangu Freedom College at Mazimbu in Tanzania (where he was accused of abusing his position of authority) and lieutenant-general in the South African National Defence Force.

In this clash of generations and clash of values, Motapanyane suffered for his beliefs, both abroad and at home. And for this his children too are to suffer, for the deeds of their parent.

A biblical harshness has fallen on this man's house. We are covered in shame.

(**Paul Trewhela:** *Political Prisoner, Pretoria Local and Central Prisons, and the Fort Prison, Johannesburg, 1964–67. Editor, Freedom Fighter (underground journal of Umkhonto weSizwe), Johannesburg, 1963–64. Co-editor, Searchlight South Africa, London (banned in South Africa), 1988–94.*)

49. *Plutarch's Lives*, Vol. 6, trans. John and William Langhorne (London: 1801), 326.
50. Daniel Roux, 'Presenting the prison: South African prison writing under Apartheid', PhD thesis (Cape Town: University of Cape Town, 2007), 6–10.
51. December 1977 was a popular month for signing the volume. Nair, Sisulu, Mbeki, Mandela, Kathrada and Toivo signed in that month, with Nair, Toivo and Mandela signing on consecutive days – the 14th, 15th and 16th, respectively. This suggests that in these cases at least, the process did not involve time for leisurely reading and reflection, but rather the marking of pre-chosen passages.
52. See the standard edition used in most universities at the time, Frank Kermode's New Arden edition of *The Tempest* (London: Methuen, 1954).
53. Although, of course, such a reading of *The Tempest* had been proposed by its readers who had been subjected by colonial rule, like George Lamming and Aimé Cèsaire. Work on the play as a postcolonial text is legion. For a representative account, see Rob Nixon, 'Caribbean and African appropriations of *The Tempest*', *Critical Inquiry*, 13 (1986): 557–78.

Chapter 2

1. Mhlangu was the first member of MK to be executed in South Africa.
2. Jeremy Cronin, *Inside and Out* (Cape Town: David Philip, 1999).
3. See Hugh Lewin, *Bandiet: Seven Years in a South African Prison*, African Writers Series (London: Heinemann, 1981).
4. www.nytimes.com/1989/05/27/world/judge-condemns-14-south-africa-blacks.html (accessed 3 December 2011)
5. Barbara Schreiner, ed., *A Snake with Ice Water: Prison Writings by South African Women* (Johannesburg: COSAW, 1992), 223.
6. An Afrikaans expression meaning 'utterly alone', literally translated as 'as solitary as a finger'.
7. See Dlamini, *Robben Island, Hell-Hole.*
8. Dennis Brutus, *A Simple Lust: Collected Poems of South African Jail & Exile Including Letters to Martha* (London: Heinemann, 1973), 56–7.
9. hopes are aborted
   dreams become nightmares
   a serene face
   twisted into distraught mask
   my ears are invaded
   by the silent clamour
   of a defeated army
   of dispirited souls.
   (James David Matthews, *Poems from a Prison Cell* (Realities, 2001)).
10. All quotations from Shakespeare are from Peter Alexander, ed., *William Shakespeare: The Complete Works* (London: Collins, 1951).
11. See http://africanhistory.about.com/od/apartheidlaws/g/No67of52.htm (accessed 1 December 2011):

    > A special court system was devised to enforce the pass law – people appearing at such 'commissioners' courts were considered guilty until they had proved their innocence. During the 60's, 70's and 80's around 500,000 Blacks were arrested each year, their cases tried (mainly uncontested), and in the 60's fined or sentenced to a short prison term. From the early 70's the convicted were 'deported' to

Bantustans instead (under the Admission of Persons to the Republic regulation Act No. 59 of 1972).

By the mid 80's, by which time almost 20 million people had been arrested (and tried, fined, imprisoned, or deported), the pass law had become increasingly difficult to enforce and it was abandoned.

12. See, for example, Dingake, 122: 'The whole of South Africa is a prison.' Dingake perceptively remarks that it was also a prison for whites, just as many Robben Island prisoners remark on the fact that the warders on the Island were as trapped as the prisoners.
13. See Stanley Cavell, *Disowning Knowledge: In Seven Plays of Shakespeare*, 2nd edn (Cambridge: Cambridge University Press, 2003).
14. Breyten Breytenbach, *The True Confessions of an Albino Terrorist* (Emmarentia: Taurus, 1984).
15. Hugh Lewin, *Bandiet: Out of Jail* (Parktown: Random House, 2002), 29.
16. See Breytenbach, for example, 'Again, I had to go through the process of stripping, and then I was counted . . .' (21).
17. Michael Neill has written to me that 'Bentham's dream was perfectly realized in the design of a convict chapel at Port Arthur in Tasmania, where each prisoner stood in a kind of upright coffin, invisible to every other prisoner, but under the constant gaze of the officiating clergyman. Prisoners in the recidivist section to which the chapel belonged were kept in silent isolation (even the guards were forbidden to speak, and wore padded slippers), and were marched to chapel wearing hoods. Any breach of regulations would result in transfer to a cell from which all light was excluded too. No wonder that the largest building in the penal settlement was the lunatic asylum.'
18. Michel Foucault, *Discipline & Punish: The Birth of the Prison*, 2nd edn (New York: Vintage, 1995).
19. Herman Charles Bosman, *Cold Stone Jug* (Cape Town: Human & Rousseau, 1981).
20. Albie Sachs, *The Jail Diary of Albie Sachs* (London: Harper Collins, 1990).
21. The topic of Hamlet's subjectivity has exercised many critics and scholars. For two recent books on the topic, see John Lee, *Shakespeare's Hamlet and the Controversies of Self* (Oxford: New York: Clarendon Press;

Oxford University Press, 2000) and Richard Hillman, *Self-Speaking in Medieval and Early Modern English Drama: Subjectivity, Discourse, and the Stage* (New York: St. Martin's Press, 1997).

22. See Emile Benveniste, 'Subjectivity in language', *Problems in General Linguistics*, Miami Linguistics Series No. 8, trans. Loiuse Meek (Coral Gables, FL: University of Miami Press, 1971).
23. Jean Middleton, *Convictions: A Woman Political Prisoner Remembers* (Randburg: Ravan Press, 1998), 102.
24. This prison cant plays on the Afrikaans term for a female animal. It also resonates with the English word 'wife' or 'wifey'.
25. Sigmund Freud, *The Uncanny* (Harmondsworth: Penguin Classics, 2003).
26. John Donne, *Meditation XVII.*
27. This is, of course, not an original observation. It has been made by many feminist Shakespeare scholars. I raise the issue here to query the exclusion of women in the Robben Island narrative, and to query the sense of what a properly realized interior self might be, for either men or women. See especially Elaine Showalter, 'Representing Ophelia: women, madness, and the responsibilities of feminist criticism', in *Shakespeare and the Question of Theory,* ed. Patricia Parker and Geoffrey Hartman (London: Methuen, 1985), 77–94.
28. Ruth First, *117 Days: An Account of Confinement and Interrogation under the South African Ninety-Day Detention Law* (London: Bloomsbury, 1989), 9.
29. Emma Mashinini, *Strikes Have Followed Me All My Life: A South African Autobiography* (London: The Women's Press, 1989), 61.
30. 'A person is a person because of other people'. This is the title of one of Jeremy Cronin's prison poems in *Inside and Out.*
31. Caesarina Kona Makhoere, *No Child's Play: In Prison under Apartheid* (London: Women's Press, 1988).
32. Long detentions, in solitary confinement, were routine for all political prisoners.
33. Dorothy Driver, 'Imagines selves, (un)imagined marginalities', *Journal of Southern African Studies*, 17.2 (June 1991): 337–54 (350).
34. John B. Bender, *Imagining the Penitentiary: Fiction and the Architecture of Mind in Eighteenth-Century England* (Chicago, IL: University of Chicago Press, 1987), 43.

35. Josephine A. Roberts, ed., *The Poems of Lady Mary Wroth* (Louisiana State University Press, 1992), sonnet 42.

Chapter 3

1. Barbara Hogan, interviewed in Barbara Schreiner, *A Snake with Ice Water*, illustrated edn (Johannesburg: Congress of South African Writers, 1992).
2. Michael Dingake, who marks Polonius's advice to Laertes, overlooks the fact that such advice is framed by the father's solicitation of spies who are instructed not only to record his activities but also actively to solicit damaging intelligence: 'Your bait of falsehood take this carp of truth' and 'By indirection find directions out' (*Hamlet*, 2.1.62 and 66).
3. For an excellent treatment of service and friendship in *Hamlet*, see Michael Neill, 'He that thou knowest thine: friendship and service in *Hamlet*', in *A Companion to Shakespeare's Works*, Blackwell Companions to Literature and Culture, ed. Richard Dutton and Jean E. Howard (Malden, MA: Blackwell Publishers, 2003), 17–20.
4. See Laurie Shannon, *Sovereign Amity: Figures of Friendship in Shakespearean Contexts* (Chicago: University of Chicago Press, 2002), 11: 'Likeness, parity, equality, and consent present a thoroughgoing antidote to hierarchies and tyrannies now (seemingly) obsolete: the likeness between friends radically cancels vertical difference.'
5. See Aristotle, *Nicomachean Ethics* (London: Prentice Hall, 1962), Book 8. Also Diogenes Laertius, *The Lives and Opinions of Eminent Philosophers* (H.G. Bohn, 1853). Aristotle 'was once asked what a friend is, and is [*sic*] answer was: "One soul abiding in two bodies"' (188), and Michel de Montaigne, *On Friendship*, Great Ideas (New York: Penguin Books, 2005).
6. See Elizabeth Hanson, 'Fellow students: Hamlet, Horatio, and the Early Modern University', *Shakespeare Quarterly*, 62.2 (2011): 205–29.
7. Colette Gordon, 'Crediting errors: credit, liquidity, performance and *The Comedy of Errors*', *Shakespeare*, 6.2 (June 2010): 165–84 (181). See also Keith Wrightson, 'Mutualities and obligations: changing social

relationships in Early Modern England', Raleigh Lecture on History, *Proceedings of the British Academy* (2006), 157–94.

8. A striking example is Mandela's laconic statement after describing Eddie Daniels's arrival on the Island: 'Eddie was to become one of my greatest friends in prison' (Kindle loc. 7334). This is never developed. Mandela speaks of Walter Sisulu as 'always being a brother to me and his friendship and support have never faltered' (Kindle loc. 3766) and of Oliver Tambo, that he is 'more than a brother to me. He is my greatest friend and comrade for nearly fifty years' (Kindle loc. 9348). But the context of this declaration is a speech which Mandela prepared, to be delivered by his daughter Zindzi, at a rally in 1985, in which he rejects the government's conditional offer of freedom. The speech continues: 'If there is anyone amongst you who cherishes my freedom, Oliver Tambo cherishes it more, and I know he would give his life to see me free. . . .' Rhetorically, the speech is similar to Marc Antony's peroration over the body of Caesar, where friendship is invoked to similarly political ends. The other man whom Mandela speaks of becoming like a 'younger brother to me' (Kindle loc. 9785) is Warrant Officer Swart, the prison officer who cooked for him and took care of him in his house at Victor Verster Prison.
9. See Desai, 24: 'I kept coming back to Hamlet, whose story of deceit, betrayal, madness and corruption had resonance for me, *especially against the backdrop of my experiences on Robben Island* . . . In "it takes from our achievements" was the recognition that there was an emerging tendency to ignobility evinced by some *in prison* that would distract from the essence of what we were striving for' (my emphasis).
10. See Transparency International, *Global Corruption Report* (Berlin: Transparency International, 2001).
11. See 'Profile: Julius Malema', BBC News Africa. Available at: www.bbc.co.uk/news/world-asia-pacific-14718226 (accessed 1 March 2012).
12. See 'Mac Maharaj and controversy: a timeline', *Mail & Guardian Online*. Available at: http://mg.co.za/article/2011–11–22-mac-maharaj-and-controversy-a-timeline/ (accessed 1 March 2012).
13. www.armsdeal-vpo.co.za/articles09/last-ditch.html (accessed 5 March 2012). The concept of 'reciprocal altruism', which comes from

evolutionary biology, was coined by R. L. Trivers to account for the peculiar ways in which an organism will minimize its own advantage at a particular moment with regard to another, in the expectation that it will benefit at a later point. See R. L. Trivers, 'The evolution of reciprocal altruism', *Quarterly Review of Biology* 46 (1971), 35–57.

14. http://allafrica.com/stories/200612180976.html (accessed 20 July 2010).
15. Although Desai claims, without providing evidence, that the first Henriad was 'read with some avidness by the inmates of the single cells' (25).
16. David Starkey, *The English Court: From the Wars of the Roses to the Civil War* (London; New York: Longman, 1987).
17. See Ernst Hartwig Kantorowicz, *The King's Two Bodies; a Study in Mediaeval Political Theology* (Princeton, NJ: Princeton University Press, 1957).
18. A copy of Mbeki's lecture is available at: www.gov.za/search97cgi/s97_cgi?action=View&Collection=speech01&Collection=speech00&Collection=speech99&Collection=speech98&QueryZip=title%3Contains%3EMbeki&SortSpec=Score+Desc&SortOrder=Descending&SortField=Score&DocOffset=198&AdminScriptName=&ServerKey=&AdminImagePath=%2Fsearch97admimg%2F. Conversations I have had with people close to Mbeki suggest that he wrote this speech himself.
19. See Sipho Seepe's extremely antagonistic account of Mkebi's fondness for quoting the classics, especially Shakespeare, and getting them wrong:

    > Always eager to display his passion for the classics, Mbeki employed Shakespeare's *The Tempest* to insult his opponents. During the Oliver Tambo Lecture at the National Institute for Economic Policy, he compared the native petit bourgeoisie and Tony Leon to Caliban and Antonio respectively. This provoked a devastating rebuke in the *Mail & Guardian* ('Mbeki misinterprets the Bard') from Howard Barrell, now this paper's editor, who holds a DPhil from Oxford University. Barrell wrote: 'For Mbeki, Prospero, the slave owner, represents the oppressed.' He continues: 'Mbeki's interpretation of the play becomes more nonsensical when he portrays Prospero's slave, Caliban, as "the native petit bourgeoisie in pursuit

> that has no object beyond itself".' He concludes: 'The quality of the research Mbeki is content to employ in insulting an opponent is abysmal'. Prominent writers from Africa and the Caribbean in whose work Prospero is cast as the colonizer would be similarly surprised at Mbeki's usage.

Available at: http://tutor.nmmu.ac.za/call/EFL/Mbeki3_illusion.htm (accessed 2 March 2012).

20. Mark Gevisser, *Thabo Mbeki: The Dream Deferred* (Johannesburg: Jonathan Ball, 2007), Kindle loc. 8696.
21. Bram Fisher was one of the lawyers who defended Mandela and others at the Rivonia trial. He was the scion of a major Afrikaans family, his grandfather having been President of the Free State Republic and his father the Judge President of the Orange Free State. He was a member of the South African Communist Party, tried for his political activities and beliefs and jailed in 1966. He contracted cancer in prison and died in 1975.
22. Hugh Lewin, *Stones against the Mirror: Friendship in the Time of the South African Struggle*, 1st edn (Cape Town: Umuzi, 2011).
23. Lewin, *Bandiet: Out of Jail*, 83.
24. Available at: http://robbenislandbible.blogspot.com/2008/11/theo-cholo.html (accessed 17 January 2012).
25. 'Tables' were small books of specially treated paper on which writing could be erased to enable new written material to be inscribed in its place. Hamlet's determination to remember the Ghost's injunctions therefore necessarily means that he has to erase, or forget, something else. See Peter Stallybrass, Roger Chartier, J. Franklin Mowery and Heather Wolfe, 'Hamlet's tables and the technologies of writing in Renaissance England', *Shakespeare Quarterly,* 55 (2004): 379–419. See also Sigmund Freud, 'A note upon the "Mystic Writing Pad"', trans. James Strachey, *International Journal of Psycho-Analysis*, 21 (1925), 469, for a psychoanalytic interpretation of the device as an analogy for the relations among perception, memory and the unconscious.
26. *The Prisoner in the Garden*, The Nelson Mandela Foundation (London: Penguin, 2005), 155–6.

Bibliography

Alexander, N., *Robben Island Dossier 1964–1974* (Cape Town: University of Cape Town Press, 1998).

Alexander, Peter, ed., *William Shakespeare: The Complete Works* (London: Collins, 1951).

Babenia, Natoo and Iain Edwards, *Memoirs of a Saboteur: Reflections on My Political Activity in India and South Africa* (Belville: Mayibuye Books, 1995).

Barber, Karin, ed., *Africa's Hidden Histories: Everyday Literacy and Making the Self*, African Expressive Cultures (Bloomington, IN: Indiana University Press, 2006).

Bate, Jonathan and Dora Thornton, *Shakespeare: Staging the World* (Oxford: Oxford University Press, 2012).

Bender, John B., *Imagining the Penitentiary: Fiction and the Architecture of Mind in Eighteenth-Century England* (Chicago, IL: University of Chicago Press, 1987).

Benveniste, Emile, *Problems in General Linguistics*, Miami Linguistics Series No. 8 (Coral Gables, FL: University of Miami Press, 1971).

Bosman, Herman Charles, *Cold Stone Jug* (Cape Town: Human & Rousseau, 1981).

Breytenbach, Breyten, *The True Confessions of an Albino Terrorist* (Emmarentia: Taurus, 1984).

Brutus, Dennis, *A Simple Lust: Collected Poems of South African Jail & Exile Including Letters to Martha* (London: Heinemann, 1973).

Buntman, Fran Lisa, *Robben Island and Prisoner Resistance to Apartheid* (Cambridge: Cambridge University Press, 2003).

Cavell, Stanley, *Disowning Knowledge: In Seven Plays of Shakespeare*, 2nd edn (Cambridge: Cambridge University Press, 2003).

Cobbett, William, *Rural Rides* (Harmondsworth: Penguin, 2001).

Cronin, Jeremy, *Inside and Out* (Cape Town: David Philip Publishers, 1999).

Daniels, Eddie, *There and Back: Robben Island, 1964–1979*, Mayibuye History and Literature Series No. 83 (Bellville: Mayibuye Books, 1998).

Deacon, Harriet, *Essential Robben Island* (Cape Town: David Philip Publishers, 1997).

— *The Island: A History of Robben Island, 1488–1990* (Belville: New Africa Books, 1996).

Derrida, Jacques, 'Living on/border lines', *Deconstructionism and Criticism*, ed. Harold Bloom et al. and trans. James Hulbert (New York: Seabury Press, 1979), 75–176.

— 'Signature event context', *Limited Inc* (Evanston, IL: Northwestern University Press, 1978).

Desai, Ashwin, *Reading Revolution: Shakespeare on Robben Island* (Pretoria: UNISA Press, 2012).

Dingake, Michael, *My Fight against Apartheid* (London: Kliptown Books, 1987).

Distiller, Natasha, *South Africa, Shakespeare, and Post-Colonial Culture* (Lewiston, NY: Edwin Mellen Press, 2005).

Dlamini, Moses, *Robben Island, Hell-Hole: Reminiscences of a Political Prisoner in South Africa* (Trenton, NJ: African World Press, 1985).

Driver, Dorothy, 'Imagines selves, (un)imagined marginalities', *Journal of Southern African Studies*, 17.2 (June 1991): 337–54.

Dutton, Richard and Jean E. Howard, eds, *A Companion to Shakespeare's Works,* Blackwell Companions to Literature and Culture (Malden, MA: Blackwell Publishers, 2003), 17–20.

Edwards, Iain, *Natoo Babenia: Memoirs of a Saboteur* (Belville: Mayibuye Books, 1995).

Ellis, Stephen, 'Mbokondo: Security in ANC camps, 1960–1990', *African Affairs*, 93 (1994): 279–98.

First, Ruth, *117 Days: An Account of Confinement and Interrogation under the South African Ninety-Day Detention Law* (London: Bloomsbury Publishers Ltd, 1989).

Foucault, Michel, *Discipline & Punish: The Birth of the Prison*, 2nd edn (New York: Vintage, 1995).

A Free Mind: Ahmed Kathrada's Notebook from Robben Island (Johannesburg: Jacana, 2005).

Freud, Sigmund, 'A note upon the "Mystic Writing Pad"', trans. James Strachey, *International Journal of Psycho-Analysis*, 21 (1925), 469.

— *The Uncanny* (Harmondsworth: Penguin Classics, 2003).

Gevisser, Mark, *Thabo Mbeki: The Dream Deferred* (Johannesburg: Jonathan Ball, 2007).

Gollancz, Israel, *A Book of Homage to Shakespeare* (Oxford: University Press, H. Milford, 1916).

Gordon, Colette, 'Crediting errors: credit, liquidity, performance and *The Comedy of Errors*', *Shakespeare*, 6.2 (2010): 165–84.

Hallengren, Anders, *Nobel Laureates in Search of Identity & Integrity: Voices of Different Cultures* (Singapore: World Scientific, 2004).

Hanson, Elizabeth, 'Fellow students: Hamlet, Horatio, and the Early Modern University', *Shakespeare Quarterly*, 62.2 (2011): 205–29.

Hillman, Richard, *Self-Speaking in Medieval and Early Modern English Drama: Subjectivity, Discourse, and the Stage* (New York: St. Martin's Press, 1997).

Isaacs, Sedick, *Surviving in the Apartheid Prison: Robben Island: Flash Backs of an Earlier Life* (Bloomington, IN: Xlibris Corporation, 2010).

Johnson, David, *Shakespeare and South Africa* (Oxford: Clarendon, 1996).

Jones, Daniel, *A Sechuana Reader* (Farnborough: Gregg, 1970).

Kantorowicz, Ernst Hartwig, *The King's Two Bodies; a Study in Mediaeval Political Theology* (Princeton, NJ: Princeton University Press, 1957).

Kathrada, Ahmed, *Letters from Robben Island: A Selection of Ahmed Kathrada's Prison Correspondence, 1964–1989* (Cape Town: Zebra Press, 2000).

— *No Bread for Mandela: Memoirs of Ahmed Kathrada, Prisoner No. 468/64*, reprint (Lexington: The University Press of Kentucky, 2010).

— *A Simple Freedom: The Strong Mind of Robben Island, Prisoner No. 468/64* (Highlands North: Wild Dog Press, 2008).

Laertius, Diogenes, *The Lives and Opinions of Eminent Philosophers* (London: H.G. Bohn, 1853).

Lee, John, *Shakespeare's Hamlet and the Controversies of Self* (Oxford & New York: Clarendon Press & Oxford University Press, 2000).

Lewin, Hugh, *Bandiet: Out of Jail* (Parktown: Random House, 2002).

— *Bandiet: Seven Years in a South African Prison*, African Writers Series (London: Heinemann, 1981).

— *Stones against the Mirror: Friendship in the Time of the South African Struggle*, 1st edn (Cape Town: Umuzi, 2011).

Lodge, Tom, *Mandela: A Critical Life* (New York: Oxford University Press, 2006).

Maharaj, Mac, ed., *Reflections in Prison*, 1st edn (Cape Town: Zebra, 2002).

Makhoere, Caesarina Kona, *No Child's Play: In Prison under Apartheid* (London: Women's Press, 1988).

Mandela, Nelson, *Conversations with Myself* (New York: Farrar, Straus and Giroux, 2010).

— *Long Walk to Freedom* (London: Holt, Rinehart and Winston, 2000).

Mashinini, Emma, *Strikes Have Followed Me All My Life: A South African Autobiography* (London: The Women's Press, 1989).

Matthews, James David, *Poems from a Prison Cell* (Athlone: Realities, 2001).

Mbeki, Govan, *Learning from Robben Island: The Prison Writings of Govan Mbeki* (London: J. Currey, 1991).

Mhlaba, Raymond, Thembeka Mufamadi, Human Sciences Research Council and Robben Island Museum, *Raymond Mhlaba's Personal Memoirs: Reminiscing from Rwanda and Uganda* (Pretoria: HSRC Press, 2001).

Middleton, Jean, *Convictions: A Woman Political Prisoner Remembers* (Randburg: Raven Press, 1998).

Montaigne, Michel de, *Montaigne: Essays* (Harmondsworth: Penguin, 1993).

— *On Friendship*, Great Ideas (New York: Penguin Books, 2005).

Naidoo, Indres, *Island in Chains: Prisoner 885/63 Ten Years on Robben Island* (Harmondsworth: Penguin, 1982).

Nixon, Rob, 'Caribbean and African appropriations of *The Tempest*', *Critical Inquiry*, 13 (1986): 557–78.

Nkosi, Lewis, *Home and Exile* (London: Longmans, 1983).

Orkin, Martin, *Shakespeare against Apartheid* (Craighall, Johannesburg: Ad. Donker, 1987).

Ostwald, Martin, *Nicomachean Ethics: Aristotle*, 1st edn (Upper Saddle River, NJ: Prentice Hall, 1962).

Pheko, S. E. M., *The True History of Robben Island must be Preserved: Robben Island Prisoners Speak* (Tokoloho Development Association, 2002).

Plaatje, Sol T., *The Boer War Diary of Sol T. Plaatje; an African at Mafeking* (Johannesburg: Macmillan, 1973).

— *Mafeking Diary: A Black Man's View of a White Man's War* (Cambridge [England]; Athens: Meridor Books, in association with J. Currey; Ohio University Press, 1990).

— *Mhudi*, Modern Classics (Johannesburg: Penguin, 2005).

— *Native Life in South Africa: Before and Since the European War and the Boer Rebellion* (Johannesburg: Ravan Press, 1982).

— *Sechuana Proverbs with Literal Translations and their European Equivalents = Diane Tsa Secoana Le Maele a Sekgooa a a Dumalanang Naco* (London: K. Paul, Trench, Trubner & Co, 1916).

— *Sol Plaatje: Selected Writings* (Johannesburg: Witwatersrand University Press, 1997).

Pogrund, Benjamin, *Sobukwe and Apartheid* (New Brunswick, NJ: Rutgers Univerity Press, 1991).

Reddy, Enuga S., 'United Nations and the international campaign against Apartheid', scnc.ukzn.ac.za/doc/AAmwebsite/AAMCONFpapers/Reddy,ES.doc.

Roberts, Josephine A., ed., *The Poems of Lady Mary Wroth* (Baton Rouge, LA: Louisiana State University Press, 1992).

Roux, Daniel, 'Presenting the prison: South African prison writing under Apartheid', PhD thesis (Cape Town: University of Cape Town, 2007).

Sachs, Albie, *The Jail Diary of Albie Sachs* (London: HarperCollins Publishers, 1990).

Sampson, Anthony, *Mandela: The Authorized Biography* (New York: Vintage, 2000).

Scarry, Elaine, *The Body in Pain: The Making and Unmaking of the World*, 1st edn (New York: Oxford University Press, 1987).

Schalkwyk, David, 'Mandela's lost manuscript: appropriation and repression in accounts of Robben Island', *Prison Writings*, ed. Danine Farquharson. www.interdisciplinarypress.net/index2.php?page=shop.product_details&product_id=190&flypage=flypage.tpl&pop=1&option=com_virtuemart&Itemid=28.

— 'Mandela's Stoicism', in *The Cambridge Companion to Nelson Mandela*, ed. Rita Barnard (Cambridge University Press, forthcoming).

— 'The rules of physiognomy: reading the convict in South African prison', *Pretexts*, 7.1 (1998): 81–96.

Schreiner, Barbara, *A Snake with Ice Water* (Johannesburg: Congress of South African Writers, 1992).

Shannon, Laurie, *Sovereign Amity: Figures of Friendship in Shakespearean Contexts* (Chicago: University of Chicago Press, 2002).

Showalter, Elaine, 'Representing Ophelia: women, madness, and the responsibilities of feminist criticism', in *Shakespeare and the Question of Theory,* ed. Patricia Parker and Geoffrey Hartman (London: Methuen, 1985), 77–94.

Smith, Charlene, *Robben Island* (Cape Town: Struik, 1997).

Stallybrass, Peter, Roger Chartier, J. Franklin Mowery and Heather Wolfe, 'Hamlet's tables and the technologies of writing in Renaissance England', *Shakespeare Quarterly,* 55 (2004): 379–419.

Starkey, David. *The English Court: From the Wars of the Roses to the Civil War* (London; New York: Longman, 1987).

Transparency International, *Global Corruption Report* (Berlin: Transparency International, 2001).

Trivers, R. L., 'The evolution of reciprocal altruism', *Quarterly Review of Biology,* 46 (1971): 35–57.

Willan, Brian, *Sol Plaatje: A Biography* (Johannesburg: Ravan, 1984).

Wrightson, Keith, 'Mutualities and obligations: changing social relationships in Early Modern England', *Proceedings of the British Academy* (2006), 157–94.

Zwelonke, D. M., *Robben Island*, African Writers Series 128 (London: Heinemann, 1973).

Index

Abrahams, Peter 12
abstract body 135–6
actor metaphor 91–2
African National Congress (ANC) 11, 26, 27, 37, 47, 67, 68, 84, 127, 165n. 4, 170nn. 46, 48
  prisoners, morale of 44
  Veteran's League 40
African Resistance Movement (ARM) 141
agency 22, 83, 92, 102, 107, 157
Alexander, Neville 16, 163n. 21, 166n. 5
  A Robben Island Dossier 152
Alexander, Peter 34, 172n. 10
Ally, Russell 30
alter ego 68, 79, 80
Anouilh, Jean
  Antigone 70–1
Anscombe, G. E. M. 168n. 27
Anthony, Frank 169n. 40
Antony and Cleopatra 16, 70, 144
Apartheid 6, 25–9, 35, 39, 43, 51, 65, 67–8, 70, 71, 81, 84, 86, 95, 129, 146, 167n. 24
Aristotle 125, 132, 142, 175n. 5
Ashcroft, Peggy 5
As You Like It 39–41, 43, 50, 64

Babenia, Natoo 47, 164n. 21, 167n. 23
Badenhorst, Colonel 164n. 24
Barrell, Howard 177n. 19
Bender, John 115, 174n. 34
Bengu, Sibusiso 47, 49
Benveniste, Emile 174n. 22
Big Fives 28
Black Consciousness Movement 47
Black homelands 81
Black Panther movement, US 47
body 2, 9, 28, 42, 54–5, 59–60, 61, 63, 68, 71, 82, 87, 95, 105, 135–7, 148, 149, 176n. 8
  see also torture
boer soldiers, and armed conflict, torture and capture 44
Bohn, H. G. 175n. 5
Book of Common Prayer (1559) 4
Bosman, Herman Charles 173n. 19
  Cold Stone Jug 88
Botha, P. W. 7, 147
breach 45–6, 173n. 17
Breytenbach, Breyten 83–5, 89–90, 95, 109, 173nn. 14, 16
  True Confessions of an Albino Terrorist 11, 62, 83
British Museum 163n. 20
brutality 28, 29, 32, 46, 51, 59, 67, 68, 79, 87, 97, 109, 139, 143, 168n. 30
Brutus, Dennis 78, 80, 95, 163n. 21, 172n. 8
Buntman, Fran 31, 46, 71–2, 166n. 10

Carlin, John 170n. 47
Cavell, Stanley 173n. 13
Cèsaire, Aimé 171n. 53
Chaplin, Charlie
  My Autobiography 15

Chartier, Roger 178n. 25
Chiba, Liloo 69, 70
Cholo, Theo 144, 153–4
Civil Rights movement, US 47
closed community, of prison 122
Cobbett, William 168n. 37
Coetzee, Dirk 167n. 24
co-mates and brothers in exile 35–43
Comedy of Errors, The 3
common humanity 42
common purpose doctrine 77
communal cell, bunk beds in 33
communal reading, in Shakespeare's comedy 43
Complete Works 34
comradeship 30, 42, 121, 127, 143
  see also friendship and struggle
Cooper, Saths 120–1, 123, 126, 127, 128, 130
  Robben Island and Prisoner Resistance to Apartheid 31
Coriolanus 16, 70, 139–40
corrupt relationship 126–8
Cronin, Jeremy 78, 172n. 2, 174n. 30
  'Death Row' 74
Cymbeline 3

Dagutt, Merton 161n. 11
Daniels, Eddie 15, 34, 164n. 21, 166n. 12, 176n. 8
Davies, Don 144
Daweti, Thompson 70
Deacon, Harriet 26, 165n. 1, 166nn. 6, 9
de Bruin, Evelina 76–7
Denmark's prison 80–3
Derrida, Jacques 21, 165nn. 1 (Introduction), 28 (Chapter 1), 169n. 39
Desai, Ashwin 17, 34, 35, 121, 164n. 22, 166n. 11, 169n. 41, 176n. 9, 177n. 15
  Reading Revolution 16, 32
Dingake, Michael 15, 17, 69, 85, 168n. 28, 173n. 12, 175n. 2
  Fight 88
displacement and repression 29–34
dispossession 55, 57–61, 72, 138
Distiller, Natasha 11, 12, 161n. 8, 169n. 41
Dlamini, Moses 79, 103, 163n. 21, 165n. 3, 172n. 7
  Robben Island 97
Donne, John 100, 174n. 26
Driver, Dorothy 112, 115, 174n. 33
Du Preez 94

Edwards, Iain 164n. 21, 167n. 23
Ellis, Stephen 169n. 44
emptiness 35, 64, 77, 86, 93, 98, 100, 108, 109, 113, 148, 157
Essop, Mohamed 43

First, Ruth 103, 105–7, 109, 111, 114, 115, 174n. 28
  117 Days 104, 114
Fisher, Bram 141, 178n. 21
Foucault, Michael 4, 81, 87, 102, 114, 115, 173n. 18
Freedom Charter 163n. 20
Freud, Sigmund 24, 99, 174n. 25, 175n. 25
friendship and struggle 120–2
  coda 152–9
  corrupt relationship and 126–8
  friends and 123–6
  isolation 139–40
  reciprocal altruism and 128–39
  twin brothers 140–52

Geloftefeesterrein 65
Gevisser, Mark 140, 178n. 20
  The Dream Deferred 139
Gollancz, Israel 168n. 36
  A Book of Homage to Shakespeare 58

Gordon, Colette 126, 175n. 7
Gqabi, Joe 61
Gqirana, Mobbs 41, 42
Gray, Stephen 55
guilt 1, 54, 63, 68, 77, 107, 157, 172n. 11

Hahn, Matthew 15, 18, 19, 20, 23, 34–6, 121, 130, 162n. 18, 164n. 27, 166n. 12
Hallengren, Anders 13, 161n. 12
Hamlet 74–8, 149, 175nn. 2–3
  burden of We and 94–103
  Denmark's prison and 80–3
  friendship in 123–6
  I/eye and 83–5
  I/You and 85–6
  lyrical *I* versus dramatic We and 78–80
  stripping concept and 86–94
  women prisoners and 103–15
Hanson, Elizabeth 175n. 6
Harris, John 141, 148, 149, 150
Hassim, Kadir 23
Heimlich 4, 99
Henry IV 129–30, 132, 133–6
Henry V 45, 47–8, 49, 56
Hillman, Richard 173n. 21
Hofmeyr, Isabel 14, 16, 161n. 14, 167n. 18
  Reading Debating/Debating Reading 13
Hogan, Barbara 96, 121–2, 175n. 1
Holliday, Tony 96
Holme, Ian 5
home, concept of 3–4

I
  and eye 83–5
  and You 85–6
  of prison 61–3
institutionality 4, 22, 41, 68, 72, 117, 122, 123
interiority 65, 89–92, 101–7, 109, 111–18
  real 91, 117
  self and 101, 104, 105, 111, 115, 174n. 27
  see also inwardness
International Convention on the Suppression and Punishment of the Crime of Apartheid 6
inwardness 89, 95, 106
  see also interiority
Isaacs, Sedick 54, 60, 63, 72, 83, 164n. 21, 168n. 29
  Surviving in the Apartheid Prison 53
isolation 12, 28, 30, 61, 77, 81, 85, 88, 95, 104, 107–12, 116, 119, 131, 139–40, 142, 157, 174n. 32
  cells 54, 60, 62, 63, 67, 83
  and privacy 105

Johnson, David 161n. 7
  Shakespeare in South Africa 11
Jones, Daniel 168n. 33
Joseph Andrews 56–7
Julius Caesar 35, 63, 64, 66, 70, 120, 143, 144, 164n. 23

Kani, John 36
Kantorowicz, Ernst Hartwig 177n. 17
Kathrada, Ahmed 16, 18, 19–20, 32, 45–6, 51, 69, 157, 162n. 17, 164nn. 21, 24, 164n. 26, 165n. 4, 171n. 51
  Letters from Robben Island 15
  No Bread for Mandela 15
Kermode, Frank 171n. 52
King Lear 34, 43, 44, 53, 55, 56, 59, 60, 61
Klerksdorp prison 111
Kroonstad Prison 27, 104, 110

Lamming, George 171n. 53
Langhorne, John 171n. 49
Langhorne, William 171n. 49
language
  significance of 93, 98
  as vehicle for self-expression 102
Lee, John 173n. 21
Leftwich, Adrian 1, 45, 141, 147, 148
Leon, Tony 138
Lewin, Hugh 86, 87, 88, 89, 94–5, 116, 142, 149–51, 172n. 3, 173n. 15, 178nn. 22–3
  Bandiet: Out of Jail 141
  Bandiet: Seven Years in a South African Prison 140
  Stones against the Mirror 141, 142, 145–8, 150
limbo, sense of being in 106
Lloyd, John 141, 148, 149
Lodge, Tom 13, 161n. 14
lyrical I versus dramatic We 78–80

Macbeth 12, 17, 39
Maharaj, Mac 49–50, 127–8, 157
Makhoere, Caesarina Kona 104, 110–12, 114, 174n. 31
  No Child's Play 110, 111, 112
Malan, D. F. 7
Malema, Julius 127, 128
Mandela, Nelson 5, 6, 11–15, 21, 25, 28–32, 36, 37, 39, 42, 46, 50–1, 64–5, 67–8, 70, 72, 74, 76, 79–80, 110, 120, 131, 138, 139, 141, 144–5, 147, 156, 161n. 10, 162n. 16, 163n. 20, 164nn. 21, 23, 165n. 4, 166nn. 8, 13, 169nn. 41–3, 170nn. 45–6, 171n. 51, 176nn. 7–8
  Conversations 51
  Long Walk 30, 47, 64, 70, 71, 80, 131–2, 142, 170n. 46
  self-control of 169n. 43
Marlowe Dramatic Society 5
Mashinini, Emma 104, 107–10, 111, 113, 115, 174n. 29
Masondo, Andrew 66–7, 68–9, 170n. 48
Matthews, James
  Poems from a Prison Cell 80, 172n. 9
Mbeki, Govan 36, 37, 138, 139, 164n. 21, 165n. 4, 166n. 13
Mbeki, Thabo 67, 127, 128, 138, 139–40, 142, 177nn. 18–19
Measure for Measure 12, 66
Merchant of Venice, The 42
Mhlaba, Raymond 165n. 4
Mhlangeni, Andrew 165n. 4
Mhlangu, Solomon 74, 76, 172n. 1
Middleton, Jean 96, 97, 174n. 23
Midsummer Night's Dream, A 3, 10, 37
Mkalipi, Kwede 19, 20, 37, 39, 42
Mkwayi, Wilton 36, 165n. 4
Mlengeni, Andrew 18–19, 20
Modisane, Blake 12, 169n. 41
Moise, David 76, 77
Montaigne, Michael de 129, 131, 132, 136, 142, 148, 175n. 5
  Essays 132
Moodley, Strini 68, 98, 170n. 47
moral order 113
moral power 114
Motapanyane 170–1n. 48
Motsoaledi, Elia 37, 39, 165n. 4
Mowery, J. Franklin 178n. 25
Mpanza, Justice 43, 44, 45
Mthembu, Jackson 163n. 20
Much Ado about Nothing 53
mutuality 32, 46, 113, 114, 118, 125, 131, 132, 134, 148

Naidoo, Indres 163n. 21, 167n. 21
Nair, Billy 72, 138, 165n. 4, 171n. 51

National Party of South Africa 26
Native Land Act (1913) 58, 81
Neal, Sylvia 162n. 17
Neill, Michael 173n. 17, 175n. 3
Nelson Mandela Foundation
Prisoner in the Garden 157, 178n. 26
New York Times 77
nihilism 35, 42, 43
Nixon, Rob 171n. 53
Nkosi, Lewis 12, 161n. 9, 169n. 41
Nzuza, J. 144

obedience 43–5, 48, 49
Okhela 84
Orkin, Martin 58, 161n. 6, 169n. 38
Shakespeare Against Apartheid 11
Othello 53
otherness 28, 53, 79, 103, 113, 114, 151

pain 36, 60, 80, 88, 89, 102, 103, 108, 116, 151, 168nn. 27, 30
humiliation and 53–4
words in 49–55, 128
Pan African Congress (PAC) 11, 26, 27, 28
Panopticon 81, 87
passivity 22, 63, 101, 103, 105
Paster, Gail 167n. 17
Pauw, Jacques 167n. 24
Pericles 3
Plaatje, Sol T. 11, 57, 60, 168nn. 31–5
Boer War Diary 58
Native Life in South Africa 58–9
Sechuana Proverbs and their European Equivalents 58
Plutarch 69
Pogrund, Benjamin 161n. 11
polis 117, 118, 122
political compromise 66
politics and friendship, relationship between 130
Polsmoor Prison 29, 85
possessiveness 71–3
Pretoria prisons 27, 74, 75, 86, 94, 95, 96, 106, 107, 111, 140, 147

Quatro 67–8, 72, 169n. 44

Rand Afrikaans University (RAU) 10, 55
rebellion and friendship 130–1
reciprocal altruism 128–39, 176n. 13
Reddy, Enuga S. 160n. 4
Redgrave, Michael 5
resistance 6–8, 12, 26, 28, 31, 41, 46, 54, 71–2, 82, 84, 106, 107, 112–13, 115, 131
failure of spirit of 52
Revenger's Tragedy, The 56
Richard II 49–51, 62, 63, 81, 94, 127
Richard III 16
Rivonia trial 6, 12, 28, 37, 64, 165n. 4, 167n. 17, 178n. 21
Robben Island 25–9
co-mates and brothers in exile in 35–43
displacement and repression in 29–34
I of prison and 61–3
men affairs and 69–71
not needing reason and 55–61
obedience and 43–5
possessiveness towards 71–3
significance of tomorrow in 34–5
stoic transcendence and guilty complicity and 63–9
TV generation and 46–9
words in pain and 49–55
see also individual entries
Robben Island Museum 29

Roberts, Josephine A. 175n. 35
room, significance of 59–60
Roux, Daniel 72, 171n. 50

Sachs, Albie 88, 173n. 20
Sampson, Anthony 13, 44, 161n. 13, 166n. 13
Scarry, Elaine 52, 59–60, 168n. 25
  Body 52–4
Schalkwyk, David 165n. 3, 169n. 43, 170n. 44
Schreiner, Barbara 97, 175n. 1
  A Snake with Ice Water 96
Schreiner, Jenny 121
Seepe, Sipho 177n. 19
self-consciousness 110, 112
self-doubt, absence of 112
self-expression 92, 101
self-government 71
selfhood 20, 22–3, 78, 79, 80, 85, 89–90, 93, 95, 98, 101, 103, 107, 108, 111, 112
  enduring 109
self-interest, reciprocal 133
self-torture 108
servitude, imposed 40, 41
sexual enslavement 97
Shaik, Mo 129
Shaik, Schabir 127, 128, 133, 137
Shannon, Laurie 131, 136, 175n. 4
Sharpville massacre 6, 26
Showalter, Elaine 174n. 27
signatures 21–4
  complexity of 22
Sijake, Sandi 39–40, 41, 167n. 16
singularity 21, 22, 23, 86
Sir Thomas More 64
Sisulu, Walter 18, 37, 42, 131, 156, 165n. 4, 166n. 13, 171n. 51, 176n. 8
Sobukwe, Robert 12, 28, 157–8
social imprisonment 116
solidarity 30, 32, 37, 46, 75, 86, 103, 121, 131, 142
  complacent 95
  social 97
solipsism 52, 83
solitary confinement *see* isolation
Solomon, Marcus 16, 32
South African Communist Party 11
South African National Defence Force 39
South African Truth and Reconciliation Commission 148, 149
South West African People's Organization (Swapo) 7
sovereign amity 136
Squires, Hilary 127, 128
Stallybrass, Peter 178n. 25
Starkey, David 177n. 16
Stoic friendship 125
stoic transcendence and guilty complicity 63–9
Strachan, Jock 152
stripping, concept of 86–94
subjectivity 11, 54, 61, 62, 78, 80–1, 103, 115, 173n. 21
  isolated 61

Table Mountain 25
tables 178n. 25
Tempest, The 3, 53, 72, 138–9, 171nn. 52–3, 177n. 19
Thambo, Oliver 170n. 46, 176n. 8
Themba, Can 12, 169n. 41
Titus Andronicus 53, 70
Toivo, Toivo ja 23, 64, 164n. 23, 171n. 51
tomorrow, significance of 34–5
Toronto Star 162n. 20
torture 44, 50–2, 63, 72, 101, 112
  see also body

transcendence 63–9, 83
Transparency International 176n. 10
Trewhela, Paul 171n. 48
Trivers, R. L. 177n. 13
Truth and Reconciliation Commission (TRC) 67
TV generation 46–9
Twelfth Night 3, 5, 36
Two Gentlemen of Verona, The 3, 142
Two Noble Kinsmen 143

Umkhonto we Sizwe (MK) 37, 43, 66, 74, 142, 170n. 46
unconscious 22, 50
United Nations General Assembly 6
University of Cape Town
  Law Race and Gender Centre 156
University of Stellenbosch 7
University of the Witwatersrand 55
University of York 55, 147

Venkatrathnam, Sonny 14, 16, 18–21, 32, 34, 46, 49, 55, 61, 63, 72, 85, 129, 155, 157, 162n. 16, 164n. 26
Venter, Sahem 162n. 19
Victor Verster Prison 176n. 8
Viktor, John 106, 107, 149, 150, 151
Vorster, B. J. 8
Vusani, J. B. 41, 42, 43

We
  burden of 94–103
  lyrical I versus dramatic 78–80
Weekly Mail, The 11
Winter's Tale, The 3
Wittgenstein, Ludwig 168n. 27
Wolfe, Heather 178n. 25
women prisoners 103–15
Woolf, Virginia 52, 168n. 25
Wrightson, Keith 175n. 7
Wroth, Lady Mary 116, 117, 118
wyfie 97

Yom Kippur war 7

Zuma, Jacob 49, 122, 127, 128, 130, 133, 137–8, 140, 142
Zwelonke, D. M. 163n. 21
  Robben Island 88